Open a Fitness Business and Make Money Doing It

Thomas Plummer

In cooperation with
International Health, Racquet & Sportsclub Association
263 Summer Street
Boston, MA 02210
(617) 951-0055
(800) 228-4772
www.ihrsa.org
www.ihrsastore.com

ISBN: 978-1-58518-046-2
Library of Congress Control Number: 2007924301

Book layout: Bean Creek Studio
Cover design: Bean Creek Studio

Healthy Learning
P.O. Box 1828
Monterey, CA 93942
www.healthylearning.com

Dedication

This book is dedicated to every brave individual who ever dreamed about opening his or her own fitness business and then took the risk to make it happen. We are in the business of changing lives, and living your dream makes the world a better place for a lot of people who might never have found fitness without you.

This book is also dedicated to the entrepreneurial spirit that has fueled the incredible growth and success of the health and fitness industry worldwide.

Acknowledgments

I can honestly say without a doubt that I have been in front of more fitness business owners and operators of every type than anyone else in the history of this industry and I think I have learned something from each and every one. Thank you to all who have passed through my seminars for the questions and experience you have brought with you.

I am also profoundly grateful that I have been able to live my life pretty much on my own terms through my involvement with the fitness industry and through the owners and vendors who have supported my efforts all these years. There are far too many to list, but to all those who have helped me along the way, I would like to say thank you once again.

This book is also the work of many people who need to be thanked. John McCarthy, former director of IHRSA and one of the legendary leaders in the industry, has given me a lot of support and encouragement over the years, and I wish to say thank you for all he has done. Several next-generation IHRSA team members, including Joe Moore and Meredith Poppler, have also given freely of their time and energy, and I am thankful for their efforts and support as well. A special thanks to the cooperation of IHRSA, especially Jay Ablondi, Vice President of Publishing; Kathleen Rollauer, Senior Research Manager; and Phoebe Anderson, Publications Coordinator.

Other IHRSA leaders, such as Joe Cirulli, Frank Napolitano, Michael Levy, and especially Tony Deleede, have also lent their support and guidance over the years and might all be surprised that some of their small comments have made a big difference in my business and success.

As I have said in my other books, no one really goes it alone. Everyone who has achieved any type of success has had the helping hand of someone else—and I am no exception. My thanks to all who have made my business and life a wonderful journey. I couldn't end this note without a special thought for Susan, who makes the journey worthwhile.

Contents

Foreword

"Common sense is not so common."

—Voltaire

For nearly 30 years, Thomas Plummer has traveled around the country, met and counseled countless health club operators, all the while building upon his knowledge of the fitness industry and dispensing his unique brand of common sense. Those who have seen him in action—and many people have, as he presents in front of more than 4,000 eager students annually—can attest that his style is his own. There is no beating around the bush with Thom. He tells it like he sees it.

Thom would be the first to tell you that some respected industry veterans disagree with certain aspects of his business model and some of his opinions. However, many successful club operators would not be where they are today had they not taken Thom's advice years ago.

Let me be clear about the purpose of this book. It is not meant to be a comprehensive reference resource on opening a health club. "Health club" is a label that can be applied to many different types of facilities. Multipurpose athletic clubs with aquatics programs and racquet sports can utilize this book, as can single-gender facilities, yoga, Pilates, and personal training studios, and many more facilities that are a blend of various activities.

What this book delivers is Thom's advice on starting and opening a successful, fitness-only health club business. Thom reports from the front lines of the industry, as his experience is cultivated from decades of interaction with successful entrepreneurs. Like the International Health, Racquet and Sportsclub Association (IHRSA), Thom is bullish on the health club industry. It is truly a great business. However, it is not an easy one. Competition can be fierce. People won't just line up to join your club. Of those people that join, many will leave. Member retention is a daily challenge, and a topic of several other publications (see the Additional Resources at the back of this book).

With this book, Thom has provided a valuable primer for aspiring entrepreneurs. It is a starting point, if you will, for your business education. It is but one course of what should become a diverse health club curriculum. Let your educational journey begin!

Yours in health,

Jay Ablondi
IHRSA, Vice-President of Publishing

1

So You Want to Open a Fitness Center?

Whatever possessed you to want to get into the fitness business? You can be sure that you will be asked this question often as you ponder opening a fitness facility for the first time. Your potential investors, your banker, your significant other, your family, and your friends will all want to know why you're getting into a business that is perceived by those on the outside as so easy, yet is known by those who own and operate fitness businesses as one of the most challenging small businesses you could own.

Opening a small business is a very serious matter that involves risk that is compounded by a high level of stress. Risk comes from that fact that you will invest your money, along with other people's cash in most cases, in a project that might fail. Failure, while not life-threatening, always feels like it at the time. Clubs fail, although in smaller numbers than the past, and the risk always exists that you will at some point have to close after losing everything you have invested.

Any small business can fail and often it is the unexpected, unknown, or emotional mistake that takes them down. The unexpected might be delays by your builder that eat up your reserve capital. The unknown might come in the form of another competitor opening in the same market that you didn't know about (because you failed to do your homework) and who chasing the same target market.

Emotional mistakes are perhaps the most frequent among young owners who become impatient and try and force the club even if it is obvious that he or she needs to back away. Taking a location that is too expensive or in the wrong part of town is a sign that you're emotional. Signing leases and other obligations when you're short of money for the overall project means that you are too emotional. Believing that it doesn't matter that 12 clubs are already in the market going after the same target members and defending that decision because you are going to build a club like no one has ever seen—and besides, you're the best trainer in town anyway—is a sign that you're making bad, emotional decisions.

The stress factor kicks in when the enormity of creating a new business where one had not existed overwhelms you in the middle of the night. You will be stressed, your family will be stressed, and people you don't even know will hate you because it will become hard to talk about anything else but your new business and how it is coming along.

"Why?" is also the most important question you should be asking yourself as you investigate getting into a new business. Why do I want to get into this? What is the expected outcome from my decision to open a fitness facility?

The expected outcome is the end result of opening your new business, usually projected five years down the road. Again, more questions will help you determine the expected outcome of your new venture. Are you opening this first unit to start a small chain and become regional? Do you plan to build up this business and then sell it at some point in the future and go on to something else? Can you build from the ground up, sell the business in the future, and hold the real estate? Is this first club all you want, as long as it can provide a good living for you and your family?

All of these questions are important and worth considering during this first phase, where you just sit back and let your imagination run wild. At this point, no limit exists to what you should be considering and all possibilities should be thought through and discussed.

One of the most important questions to consider during this "What if I opened a fitness center?" stage is that of lifestyle versus risk. Someone pursuing lifestyle, for example, is not always someone who makes a successful business owner.

Lifestyle people are those who love working out everyday or might be personal success stories when it comes to fitness. These folks are the ones who have lost the extreme weight, battled through an unhealthy situation in their life, or have had fitness somehow be a life-changing experience. These people are passionate and want to share with the world what fitness has done for them and they see opening a fitness center as the best avenue to reach that goal.

These people often have the hardest time in the fitness business as owners and operators because they enter a very demanding field least prepared for the business aspects. The fitness business is truly rewarding in that you have the chance to change lives every day, but the business skills, such as raising capital, managing a staff, mastering marketing and sales, and developing programming all have to be in place for that new business to survive and prosper in a competitive market.

Risk is the other side of the lifestyle coin. As mentioned earlier, opening any new business is always accompanied by the prospect that the business might fail. Your job as you consider getting into the fitness industry as an owner is to minimize this risk by learning as much as you can about how the business works, acquire the skills you need as a businessperson to succeed, and go into your new company with your eyes open to the risk involved in betting your money, and usually someone else's money as well.

Look at other clubs carefully and learn to see beyond the pretty equipment and classes. What basic business principles enable one club to succeed where others merely survive? What "best practices" separate financially successful club owners from those that flail away at the business, never really making any money?

Lifestyle is the benefit of being in this industry, but the only way you will succeed financially over time is to understand that it is a business and that you are willing to run it as such every single day you own it. People call them gyms, clubs, and training centers, but the real term you need to understand is that they are all fitness businesses, with the operative word being "business."

If lifestyle is your ultimate choice, meaning that you want to get into the fitness business because you love to work out or you want to share your personal fitness success with others, then you might be better off working in a club as a trainer or some type of other fitness professional. But if you're like Braham Akradi, founder of Life Time Fitness (NYSE: LTM), the last fitness group to go public; Joe Cirulli, owner of several financially successful fitness centers in Florida; or Joe Millet, managing partner of the Big Sky chain in Connecticut, you can figure out how to be both financially successful and enjoy the fitness lifestyle. All three of these outstanding business professionals started small and grew into major players, either nationwide or in their respective areas, and all started with a love for fitness that they maintained long after their success was secured.

What sets these three business owners apart, and many other men and women like them, is that they had a love for the fitness business but also took the time to develop themselves as businesspeople along the way. In the end, to be successful in this business you have to have both a passion for helping people and changing lives and the drive to master all aspects of the business itself.

In the end, to be successful in this business you have to have both a passion for helping people and changing lives and the drive to master all aspects of the business itself.

Common Mistakes

As you take your first step into the world of owning a fitness business, be aware of the common mistakes you can make at this stage that will negatively affect the outcome of your business later. These mistakes are not the only ways that you can end up in trouble, but they are definitely shared by the largest percentage of new fitness owners.

Sticking with the wrong concept. Many people latch on to a concept and then won't let it go, even if it doesn't really fit them or their market. For example, you might have dreamed of opening your own training center specializing in upscale adults, but if three or four of these are already in your marketplace, you must decide if the area can support another one. Forcing a concept will almost always end in financial failure. Can you take your concept to another market that is underserved or can you change your plan and perhaps open a women-only gym or a speed school for children, which may be underserved in your town?

Overpaying for someone else's dream or mistake. It is amazing how many people get into the fitness business after being drawn in by someone else's passion. This happens often, for example, when a passionate trainer hooks up with a client (the money person) to open a new center. The trainer hasn't taken the time to learn how a business works as a business and the money person trusts his trainer to know the business because the trainer has done so much to help the client. In this scenario, the investor will often end up with the business because the trainer, who was never prepared to run the business, can't make money and walks away, leaving the person who signed for the money and the lease behind in the fitness business. Are you opening this facility because it is a good business plan or because you're caught up in some else's dream?

Doing it for the wrong reason. As mentioned earlier, if you're opening this new business because you just want a place to work out that's better than the other places in your town, or because you love the dream of changing hundreds of lives the way yours changed when your first discovered the wonders of working out, then you're doing it for the wrong reasons. Can you take this passion and make money with it? That question is the most important thing to ask yourself at this stage.

Being too emotional. It is not unusual for a person to rush too quickly when first thinking about opening a fitness facility. A common mistake, for example, is to put together a little money and look for first location. The first location isn't exactly right and might be lacking the right amount of parking or be too much rent, but your passion gives you a sense of urgency and you force your new business into something that will increase your chances of failure later. It is hard to do, but set your emotionalism aside and remember that it's a business you're opening, and that you need to be able to walk away from any deal that doesn't make sense in your business plan or that has to be forced to make happen.

So, why do you want to get into the fitness business? If you're creating a practical business plan and are willing to learn all the aspects needed to be financially successful over time, then you will make it. If, on the other hand, you're opening this business because working out everyday in your own place, standing at the counter greeting your members, and thinking you will hire the experts you need to actually run the place while you train people is your dream, then getting a job in a fitness business might be a much more practical idea than actually owning one.

Focusing Your Project

At some point, you have to turn your dream into the first few steps of reality. The expected outcome is to take that vague idea of owning a fitness business and start to give it a shape, a rough cost, a target market for your new business, and to find out if owning a small business is the avenue you want to pursue to realize your dream of working in the fitness industry for a living.

Giving your dream a shape and a focus early also allows you to have those initial talks with bankers or investors, and lets you start to develop an initial cost factor. You may be dreaming, for example, of opening a large multipurpose club, but after spending time developing your initial focus, you might find that your interests, or your capital, push you in another direction.

Going in with a focus up-front also can save literally hundreds of thousands of dollars later in the project by eliminating costly wrong turns, such as investing too much money too soon and then finding out you don't have the funding or support you need to finish the project. Even the money you will spend on a business plan, a vital tool to raise money and to develop a working concept, can be wasted if you don't have an idea going in about what you want and can afford.

Think these points through thoroughly and start to build your project notebook based upon your thoughts and research. Most of the ideas defined in this chapter will also be covered in depth in other chapters. Again, all you're trying to do at this point is start developing a firmer concept of your new business. Ask yourself the following questions:

- Can my community support another fitness facility?
- What is my target market for this club?
- Can I find a home for my business by becoming a specialist?
- Should I attempt to make this a real estate project or is renting my best option?
- Success in other businesses doesn't always guarantee success in this one. What do I need to learn in this business to be successful?

- Do I really know what I am getting into with this business? Do I understand that this is a seven-day-a-week business that is capital-intensive and will have all the staff and member problems associated with opening any type of service business?

- Am I aware of how long it takes to actually open a new business? Have I thought about how long it takes to raise capital, get permits, use an architect, and build my new business?

Can your community support another fitness facility?

An interesting thing about fitness centers is the true market area they command. Most new owners go into their projects looking at their marketplace as being much bigger than it really is, when in reality your market is always smaller than you think. Consider the following: 85 to 90 percent of your membership will most likely come from within a 12-minute drive time of your club.

For most clubs, this drive time translates into a three- to five-mile ring from the proposed site. You can figure this out without being too scientific. Find the area of town you are thinking about, pick a street corner, and then, at about 6:00 p.m., which should be rush hour for most markets, drive 12 minutes in one direction and mark that spot on a map. Then go back to your corner and head out in another direction for 12 minutes. Eventually, you will build a rough circle around that site that highlights your potential market.

This low-tech method will determine how hard it would be for your potential members to get to your club. Once you establish a ring, you can mark off competitors that would be in your competition area and get an idea about how many different clubs are in your ring. Also try and establish the target market for each one of these competitors.

IHRSA provides some great information about club usage hours for different types of business models. Keep in mind that your club will probably be a little different due to the types of businesses in the area, density, and number of competitors.

Most new owners go into their projects looking at their marketplace as being much bigger than it really is, when in reality your market is always smaller than you think.

What is your target market for this club?

When you think about your target market, you're trying to determine who will use your club. When asked whom their club is for, many rookie owners respond with somewhat vague answers. "Well, it's for people with money," or "I'm going to specialize in older people," or "I'll have something for everyone."

Target market is defined as the core 80 percent of your membership. In other words, about 80 percent of your membership may come from one specific target market. This market usually encompasses about two generations, although you obviously will have a large number of members over or under your target age.

For example, you might be an upscale adult club that has a target market of 30 to 50 years old with average household incomes of over $60,000. In this example, about 80 percent of your members would be in this age category.

An important thing to remember is that likes attract likes. In other words, people like to socialize and hang out with people like themselves. Therefore, knowing your target population is important because every decision you will make, from the color of the paint to the programming choices in your business, should be based upon acquiring members in your target group.

Can you find a home for your business by becoming a specialist?

If three good pizza places were on three corners of a busy intersection, would you open another pizza place on the fourth corner or would you consider opening a burger place or Chinese restaurant? Specializing, or finding a niche, is nothing more than trying to determine which segments of your market are being served by existing clubs, and which areas or target populations are underserved. For example, if your area has four or five clubs all vying for the same 18-to-34-year-old market, would it make sense to open another club that goes after those same demographics or would you be better off to open an upscale adult club, women-only facility, or perhaps a lifestyle enhancement center (personal training center)?

Specializing is also usually cheaper than trying to open a big box–style club. Many markets don't have the square footage available to develop a large facility, yet many of these same markets could benefit from smaller facilities that are going after more narrowly defined target markets.

The question to ask yourself is as follows: Are more narrowly defined markets available, such as sports performance for children or women-only clubs that would make sense in my market, rather than opening a typical box club that needs more capital and is already been done in my desired area? Another way to look at this situation is: Can I specialize in a specific niche and still make money?

Should you attempt to make this a real estate project or is renting your best option?

Building from the ground up is often an option that is not considered by a new fitness-business owner, but you should take a look at this option, especially if you have investors and the right market. Most people thinking about getting into the fitness business start with rental space, assuming that it will be cheaper and easier to get into initially. Rental space, however, can often be harder to get into because of the collateral needed to get the project funded through traditional sources and because of the difficulty of attracting investors.

For example, an upscale club of 10,000 square feet could cost as much as $1.3 million to build based upon the following numbers, which are averages for this type of club. In some markets you might be able to build for less or have a lower rent factor, which would affect the operating cost per month as well the reserve.

- Build-out for the interior at $50 (not common anymore) to $60 or $70 per foot (becoming the new standard) = $600,000
- Equipment = $300,000 (heavy on cardio and functional)
- Reserve capital = $225,000 (three months reserve at $75,000 per month operating expense)
- Miscellaneous = $75,000 (computers, software, stock and inventory, licenses and certifications, etc.)
- Architectural fees = $80,000
- The total for this project would be $1,280,000 and you would need at least $250,000 to $400,000 in cash (depending on the bank) to make it happen.

In this example, you have two problems to consider. First of all, a banker may want you to have at least 20 percent down for this project for traditional financing and you would have to collateralize the balance at 80 to 100 percent. In other words, the bank might give you the money, but you have to put up real property or other collateral, such as stocks or CDs, which have to cover at least 80 percent of the money you borrow.

The reason the banker has this requirement is that if you fail the bank has nothing to go after because everything you spend the money on, such as build-out and equipment, really doesn't have any value to the bank. The build-out stays with the building and is the property of the owner of that building, and the equipment is hard to sell for any real money. In other words, you have nothing the bank can seize to liquidate to get their money back.

The second issue it that this scenario is difficult to use to attract investors. You're in essence asking your money people to get into the fitness business with you, which is something most don't want to do. This type of business might provide a great living for you, but paying back investor money with a decent interest rate puts extra strain on the business. Investors are usually looking for a way to make a good return on their money and want the principle back in a decent amount of time rather than acting like a bank that might be willing to structure the debt over a longer time and at a lower interest.

The investor is also faced with the same issue that the bank is: What happens to his money if you fail? Again, nothing would be available to go after that is worth selling off to pay back the debt. If you fail, everyone loses, which is why putting this much money into rental space is so hard for many potential owners.

On the other hand, it is a lot easier to attract people who want to be in real estate. Even the banks like real estate projects more than they like rental space in many towns, because if you fail something concrete exists that can be sold to pay back the money that was borrowed.

Investors especially like to be in the real estate investment business. If the plan looks good, an investor can put some cash in and then the investment becomes passive, meaning that he can go after other projects instead of being tied up with this one. He also gains equity over time, appreciation in the real estate, and is probably also getting a return on his investment as well.

The problem is that many potential owners never consider real estate because the number is too big and it scares them. For example, that same 10,000-square-foot club might cost $2.7 to $3.0 million to build from the ground up based on these general figures:

- Land = $800,000 (an acre-and-a-half minimum in most areas)
- Site preparation = $100,000 (prepare the site, retention ponds, utilities)
- Shell of the building = $700,000 (based on $70 per foot)
- Build-out = $600,000 (based on $60 per foot)
- Equipment = $300,000
- Architect = $150,000
- Reserve = $225,000 (three months based on $75,000 monthly operating expense)
- Miscellaneous = $75,000
- The total for this project would be approximately $2,950,000.

Sticker shock is high when you ask a potential owner to consider this number, but again, this project might be easier to complete in many markets. First of all, the Small Business Administration (SBA) has certain programs, such as the 504, that make getting into this type of project much easier. These programs are handled through banks that specialize in working with the SBA and usually only require 10 to 15 percent down. Raising $270,000 to $400,000 might be easier than coming up with the same amount of money and then still having to come up with the collateral to cover the rest of your loan using the rental space example.

This project could also be tweaked a little to increase investor potential by adding 10,000 square feet of rental space on the first floor and putting the fitness facility on the top floor. If the rental space were done well, and in the right location, the rents for the first floor would offset a great deal of the monthly debt for the entire project.

In the real estate example, if the project turned out to cost $3 million, and the owner raised $500,000 through investors looking for a real estate project, the monthly payment would only be about $18,000 for everything, which would be largely offset by having 10,000 square feet of rental space available.

The final point in this debate is that the owner in the rental space might be paying $10,000 to $14,000 for rent alone in his space, not counting debt service to the bank, while the owner in the second example might be paying just $18,000 per month for the entire project, not counting offsets for the retail space that could be rented.

As you focus your project, consider building or buying an existing building if it fits your market. You might find it easier to get a bank to work with you or to find needed investors who would rather own real estate rather than a fitness center.

Success in other businesses doesn't always guarantee success in this one. What do you need to learn in this business to be successful?

Every business has it's own nuances, needed skill sets, and learning curve. Being a competent businessperson in another area obviously does give you an edge when getting started, but the rules are different and many experienced businesspeople are surprised when they find that the fitness business looks so easy on the outside but is so difficult once you own your own facility.

When you consider opening a fitness business, you don't need all the answers, but you do need to understand the questions, and these questions come from understanding all the moving parts of a typical fitness business. These areas of needed expertise are as follows:

- Management and numbers: How does a club make money? How do you collect money from your members? What is a good payroll percentage? How do you market to attract enough leads to drive your business? Why do clubs fail and how can you avoid these mistakes? All of these questions, especially those that pertain to the financial foundation of the business, have to be answered before you build your first business plan. You must also consider the question: Who is going to run the backshop part of your new business on a daily basis?

- Working people out: Fitness is your base product. Who can certify your trainers? How do you find and hire trainers? What is current in the training field? What is the culture you need to establish that will help the largest percentage of your members get results and achieve success? Building a successful fitness program is not a random act and it takes thought to match your club's offerings and programming with your target market.

- Weight management: More than 60 percent of the American population is overweight. The fitness business has to provide leadership in this area in the future to further expand its penetration to reach new folks who don't yet use a fitness facility.

- Customer service and staffing: Member retention and staffing will be the two biggest issues in the fitness business during the next 10 years. How do you keep the members you get? How do your find and develop a staff that can drive revenue in your business? How do you pay employees and keep them motivated over time?

- Sales: Selling memberships and services are always going to be part of owning a fitness facility. In fact, sales can be defined as follows: 95 percent of what you do every day is sell somebody something. The other 5 percent involves management of the business. A fitness business is a production-based business that depends on daily cash flow, which only comes from selling new memberships and services in the business.

As a potential owner of a fitness business, you need to have a grasp of all of these skills, especially when it comes to sales. You can hire expertise to cover your weak areas, but you have to have a working idea yourself if you want to be successful. In sales, for example, you would find it hard to hire and manage a sales team if you have never sold memberships yourself in a fitness business—and the same is true for the other skills. You don't have to be an expert, but you do have to have a working concept concerning all the main parts of a typical fitness business.

Do you really know what you are getting into with this business? Do you understand that this is a seven-day-a-week business that is capital-intensive and will have all the staff and member problems associated with opening any type of service business?

How hard could it really be to own a fitness business? You get to work out anytime you want. You get to hang out with fit, good-looking people. Everyone wants to work in a fitness business so staff shouldn't be an issue.

Opening a fitness business is like opening any other customer-service business. You will have to put in a lot of hours and hard work, especially during the first year, to make it work.

The fitness business is also capital-intensive, meaning that it costs a lot more to open than many other small businesses you might consider. Reinvestment is also a considerable cost over time.

Opening a small business is often a surprise for many people. You must enter your new business with the understanding that owing a fitness business has a unique set of challenges and that you've just bought yourself the right to put a lot of hard work into your dream.

Are you aware of how long it takes to actually open a new business? Have you thought about how long it takes to raise capital, get permits, use an architect, and build your new business?

The lengthy timeline is often the biggest surprise of all for potential owners, especially those that think opening a new business will take only a few months. Look at this typical timeline for opening in rental space. It represents an average, but does cover all the stages you'll go through on your journey:

- Getting a focus and conceptualizing your business: 1 to 2 months
- Writing a business plan: 2 months
- Working with banks and investors to raise capital: 3 months
- Negotiating rental space: 1 to 2 months
- Using an architect and acquiring permits: 2 months
- Build-out: 4 to 6 months

From the moment of, "Hey, I want to get into the fitness business," to the moment of "Welcome to my new place," may take anywhere from a year to 18 months in a rental-space facility. If you want to build, it will take at least a year and maybe as long as two if you encounter any code issues in your area or need to attract more than one investor into your new real estate project.

If you have capital already in place and an inventory of space in your area to choose from, then you might get it done in as little as nine months, but that is quicker than normal for most projects. The key is to not be surprised about the length of time and don't force the project because of the emotional need to get it done in a hurry and get in and working. All projects have a natural flow and the most common mistake is to go too quickly and make bad decisions that cost you time and that hurt your business once you're open.

Build It to Sell It

Every decision you make should enhance the ultimate value of your business, because at some point you are going to want to get out. It might seem a little backward, but many owners are more successful because they get in with a plan to get out, and that plan is based upon getting the maximum dollars for their business.

For example, if you build in rental space, as mentioned earlier, you will have to sign a lease with the landlord for your new business. The length of the lease, the option periods, the value of the lease compared to market value, and any build-out you might negotiate all can affect the value of the business when you sell in the future, because having the right to perpetuate the business into the future at a below-market rate is much more valuable then buying a standard lease with limited options.

The Key Concept in This Chapter

At some point, you have to take the steps necessary to turn your dream of being in the fitness business into reality. The first step is to start take all of those random ideas and focus them into one set concept that fits you and your market. Be open to new ideas and don't force a concept because of being too emotional. Opening a small business is a big step in most people's lives and you want to give yourself every chance to be successful, both financially and in your dream to help people change their lives for the better through fitness.

Additional Resources

McCarthy, J. (2004). *IHRSA's Guide to the Health Club Industry for Lenders and Investors* (2nd ed.). Boston, MA: IHRSA.

2

Conceptualizing Your
New Business

The first step in conceptualizing your business is asking yourself, "Who is this business for?" The fitness business has been around since approximately 1945 in its present form, defined as clubs for the public based upon membership sales. Clubs existed prior to that date, but the fitness business really began to take off in the late 1940s and early 1950s.

After all these years, the industry has only managed to capture 16 percent of the population according to IHRSA research. In other words, after more than 60 years, only 16 percent of the people in America belong to fitness centers. The industry has done a decent job of attracting people who are interested in fitness, but it hasn't yet done the work necessary to attract the other 84 percent who don't belong to any type of fitness facility.

Industry insides call these groups the "Get Its" and the "Don't Get Its." Those who understand fitness and the importance it can play in their lives—those who get it— already work out and belong to fitness clubs. The rest don't yet make the connection.

The mistake club owners make, and the opportunity of the future, is that almost everything they do in their clubs is targeted at people who get fitness and understand it, and almost nothing is really aimed at those who don't yet get it.

Who are the "don't get it" people and what do they want from you?

Start with the premise that about 300 million people live in this country. Out of this number, roughly 45 million belong to fitness facilities of some type. IHRSA research shows that approximately 30 million more may have belonged to a fitness center at some point in their lives, but currently do not.

Using these numbers, approximately 225 million potential members are out there who have not participated in a fitness facility. If the industry only converted 5 percent, or 11.25 million, it could change the very nature of what you do for a living. Divide that number by the 29,000 mainstream fitness centers in America, as of 2006, and every gym currently in business would get 387 new members, a significant number for most clubs.

Where club owners go wrong is that they try to change the world by going too big too soon. Not everyone is a fitness candidate and not everyone will join a gym. You need to think about the fitness business as more of a continuum, with those who will never, ever join fitness centers on the extreme left and the hard-core workout fanatics on the extreme right. Figure 2-1 depicts this continuum, including the 16 percent that represents all current club members. You live and work on the right side and your potential markets are those closest to that side.

According to IHRSA, the number of people joining gyms has slowly been rising at a rate at about 5 percent per year. That growth, and the future of the industry, will come from those folks closest on the continuum to the 16 percent number. These are the folks who fit the rest of your demographics and who sort of understand what you do, but for whom fitness hasn't yet become important in their lives.

An example is a former housewife who has raised her kids, returned to the workforce at age 40, and now wants to spend some time working on herself. She might have never belonged to a gym, but she is a strong candidate because she has everything you need: awareness, income, education, and opportunity.

The challenge is to take advantage of this opportunity in your market by building facilities and creating a business plan that goes after this group. The fitness people already in the market will find you, but future success lies in developing new markets that are being underserved.

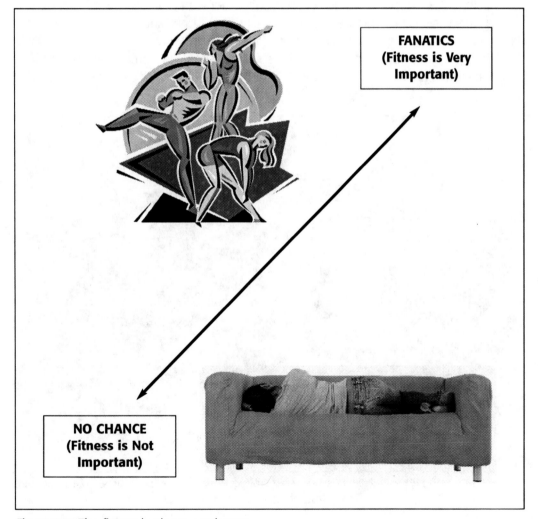

FANATICS
(Fitness is Very
Important)

NO CHANCE
(Fitness is Not
Important)

Figure 2-1. The fitness business continuum

How big is your potential market?

Capture rate is the term that defines how much of your market you should be able to acquire as members in your club. The problem with any type of capture-rate formula is that it is hard to develop just one formula that covers every type and size of facility and price structure. For example, a 10,000-square-foot club and a 40,000-square-foot club in a market of 50,000 people, using a set capture rate of 4 percent, would both come up with answers that would be unrealistic for their business plans.

Remember from Chapter 1 that your market is within an approximate 12-minute drive time from the club during rush hour. The 4 percent number would mean that each club in this market would capture 2,000 members, which is probably too high for the smaller club in most markets, yet too low for the larger club to survive.

Again, price structure, profit centers, and other competition are all factors that would affect the actual numbers that each club would get and need to survive over time. For example, the smaller club might have an extremely low price, which would lead to larger sales numbers and memberships, but would at some point mean that it might become unable to sustain those numbers due to market saturation and loss rates.

Capture rate is the term that defines how much of your market you should be able to acquire as members in your club.

Determining Market Potential

Two methods can be used to help get an idea of your market potential. The first is a sliding scale and the second is based upon actual expenses in the club. Both represent the minimum numbers you need to make the business work.

It is important to know when you have to hit these numbers. The most important month in your business is the twenty-fifth, which is when your business plan should mature and when you reach the target number of new members that your club needs to be financially successful. You don't have to wait this long, however, to start making money.

Most clubs can cover their own expenses somewhere during the seventh to ninth month of operation, assuming that the club opened somewhere between August 15 and February 15 and has at least two months of operating capital in reserve. If you open your club in May or June, which is the hardest time period to open a new facility in most markets, your new business won't come together until about the tenth month and you will need a full three months of operating reserve.

Method 1: Percentage of population

This method is based upon square footage and the percent of the population in your 12-minute drive time that you can capture. It is a sliding scale and represents the minimum number of members you need to have in your system paying during the twenty-fifth month of operation.

Again, the twenty-fifth month is important because it reflects the full maturation point for a typical club. You've had two full years of business and are now entering your third year. By this point, your club has passed through two full member-retention cycles and your net receivable check should be at its highest point. At this point in time, this check should be covering at least 70 percent of your base operating cost each month, with an ultimate target of 100 percent coverage.

Your total membership at this point is also important. Loss rates and retention rates are known and often your membership at this point reflects the highest point possible in your club. It is possible to increase membership beyond this point, but the combination of losses and retention issues often flatten the membership growth at this point.

The example presented in Figure 2-2 is based upon a market of 50,000 people in a five-mile ring from the club, or about 12 minutes of driving time, and the target number represents memberships and not the total number of actual members. Keep in mind that memberships represent a single financial instrument to be collected by the club, but this membership might have more than one person included. For example, you might generate a membership for a husband and wife, which represents one membership but two members. The calculation is based on using the multiplier as a derivative of the total population. In this case, the multiplier is percentage of the population you can hope to attain as memberships in your new club.

Total Square Footage	Total Population	Multiplier	Target Members	
5,000	50,000	x .015	750	(50,000 x .015 = 750)
10,000	50,000	x .025	1250	(50,000 x .025 = 1250)
15,000	50,000	x .03	1500	(50,000 x .030 = 1500)
20,000	50,000	x .035	1750	(50,000 x .035 = 1750)
25,000	50,000	x .04	2000	(50,000 x .040 = 2000)
40,000	50,000	x .05	2500	(50,000 x .050 = 2500)
50,000	50,000	x .06	3000	(50,000 x .060 = 3000)
60,000	50,000	x .07	3500	(50,000 x .070 = 3500)
75,000	50,000	x .08	4000	(50,000 x .080 = 4000)

Figure 2-2. Percentage of population

Method 2: Sales needed compared to operating expenses

This method, based on what is called the one per thousand rule, bases your total needed memberships upon the monthly memberships you need to sell compared to what it costs you to run your facility each month, and then factors in price. This rule may be the single, most important concept in the fitness business because if you break this rule you will have a hard time surviving.

One of the most frequently asked questions by a potential owner developing a business plan is: How many new members do I have to get each month to make it? Looking at needed monthly sales allows you to get a feel for if your business plan sounds logical for your market. For example, if you live in a town of 20,000 people, but your expenses are $80,000, you might need more members per month than your market can handle.

Keep in mind that expenses are situational. The rent factor, or mortgage number, may be substantially lower in some markets, thereby lowering your overall operating expenses. For example, you might spend $6 per square foot in a southern market as compared to $48 a square foot in a major metro market such as San Francisco.

Your expenses may also vary due to the type of club you choose. For example, the interior finish and operating expense for a 25,000-square-foot women-only club in Boston may be twice as much as that of a lesser club in a more rural market in the same state. Lower-end clubs basing their business plan on volume, such as those in the $19 per member per month category, often will have less monthly expense than a full-service club with a full array of group classes and a full staff of trainers.

> The one per thousand rule is stated as follows: You need one new annual membership per every thousand dollars of expense per month to survive, based upon a price of $39 per month.

This rule is based upon the new, annual memberships, either contractual or paid-in-full, you generate each month. This rule does not include renewal members or account for short-term memberships. Your goal as an owner is to average the needed number over the last three-month period in your business, because in the fitness business you might get 150 new members in March, but only 30 in July.

To calculate this number, divide your cost of operation by the number closest to your monthly price, as depicted in Figure 2-3. For example, if your expenses are $70,000, and your anticipated price is $39 per month for an individual membership, then divide $70,000 by 1000. In this example, you will need 70 new members on average per month to become financially successful.

If your price is:	Total Monthly Expenses	Divide Cost of Operation by:	Minimum Number of Monthly Members	
$19	$70,000	600	116	($70,000/600)
$29	$70,000	800	87	($70,000/800)
$39	$70,000	1000	70	($70,000/1000)
$49	$70,000	1200	58	($70,000/1200)
$59	$70,000	1400	50	($70,000/1400)
$69	$70,000	1600	43	($70,000/1600)
$79	$70,000	1800	38	($70,000/1800)
$89	$70,000	2000	35	($70,000/2000)

Figure 2-3. The one per thousand rule

This rule does not account for profit centers, which generate money on top of these sales numbers. It also does not take into account-retention numbers. This rule simply gives you the minimum number you need to average each month in new, annual memberships to stay in business. If you hit these numbers, you have a good chance of surviving and even being financially successful. If you consistently fall short, your chance of failure is higher.

Remember, in the fitness business, hardly anyone fails during their first year or so. The analogy is that you don't die in this business from a brick to the head, but rather from running naked through a rose bush—it takes you four years or so to slowly bleed to death. This slow death comes from never hitting your minimum sales numbers, although if you are close each month, you can hang on for several years before you are finally forced to close.

Sales are your life blood in the business, and when you conceptualize your business plan, you need to start with getting an understanding of how many sales, and how many new memberships, your business will need. Then you must determine if those sales are reasonable for the type of club you are considering opening in your market.

Sales are your life blood in the business, and when you conceptualize your business plan, you need to start with getting an understanding of how many sales and new memberships your business will need.

Where Is the Growth Going to Be in the Future?

When you start to conceptualize your new club, you have to consider your market and what it would take to compete. Markets can be divided into four distinct subgroups. Each group, or level, includes certain types of clubs that would work in it, but might not work in others.

Level 1 markets

Level 1 markets are the major metro markets that have 250,000 residents or more. During the past years, the large chains have been aggressive in these types of cities, often opening on the same street in the same part of town.

Rent factors are usually high, which limits your space and the type of club you might want to open. If you want to get into this type of market, such as Denver proper or Chicago, you may want to find a niche and think nontraditional. It is hard to get the space you need at a rent that makes sense, so independent owners open target specific clubs, such as hybrid training centers or upscale women's clubs. They also put clubs high up in buildings where the rent might be lower or look for basement space.

Hybrid training centers are defined as small clubs, usually in the 1,500 to 5,000 square-foot range, that specialize in training but also offer memberships on a limited basis. These clubs are a more advanced version of the old personal training studios that were too dependent on too few people to survive.

Level 2 markets

Level 2 markets are the suburban markets or smaller population cities, with populations in the 100,000 to 250,000 range. The chains are beginning to expand into these areas as the level 1 markets become saturated, but a lot of growth potential is still available if you find the right area.

These markets can support the larger clubs, such as the 40,000-square-foot boxes, but smaller clubs that go after narrower niches can also do well, such as 12,000-square-foot women-only facilities. The franchise clubs, such as AnyTime Fitness® or Gold's Gym®, also do well in these markets because they can vary their size to suit space concerns. Some of the newer franchises, such as Planet Fitness®, also do well in certain segments of these markets that have strong turnover and density.

Level 3 markets

Level 3 markets have 50,000 to 100,000 residents and may be one of the last great club markets left. Operators already exist in these markets, but many are old and out of date and a newer operator with a more modern concept can often do well.

Depending on the actual size of the market, smaller clubs in the 7,500-to-15,000-square-foot range do well and space is usually available at a reasonable cost, although in a large segment of level 3 markets, a 25,000-square-foot club would also work. You can also buy a building lot in these markets and build your own fitness center/retail space using the concept discussed in Chapter 1 where it describes a combination of retail space on the ground floor with a fitness facility upstairs.

The chains aren't likely to hit these areas too hard because they often don't fit their model or going-public plans, giving an aggressive local owner a chance to open a small, regional chain or to open with vertical segments in mind, which means that you open a variety of clubs with different names that target different groups. Doing so ties up the market to new competition. You might, for example, open a mainstream fitness facility under one name and a women-only club three miles away under a different name, giving the illusion to outsiders that the market is full.

Level 4 markets

These markets have fewer than 50,000 people—small-town America at its best. These markets are great, and clubs that are successful are often the only game in town. These clubs are lifestyle facilities, where you pick this town because you grew up there or because you really want to live there.

Clubs in these markets often get a bigger market share because they fulfill a more social role in the community and become the place to hang out and see people. This market is also underserved, with many small towns only having an old, storefront type of club.

Newer clubs, with group fitness, a pool, and multipurpose rooms that can be rented out to the public, would do well in these communities. Clubs in towns this size that have a large number of tourists also do well if they focus on their two separate markets: the locals who support the club year-round and the tourists who hit it hard during limited seasons.

Building a Gym for a Specific Target Market

You can't be everything to everyone in the fitness business anymore. Multipurpose facilities that cater to the masses are getting scarce, and those that are being built are usually beyond the financial means of most people trying to get into the fitness business as individuals.

Before you open, you have to have a specific target market in mind. This target market is based upon age and affluence. Remember that likes attract likes, and successful clubs in the future will be built upon more narrowly defined populations that share common interests and desires. For example, the programming in a club for those who are 24 to 40 years old would be much different from that in a club that specializes in members who are 35 to 55 years of age.

The common response to this viewpoint is that you can offer programming for everyone in the same facility by just changing classes. But do all of those different groups really want to belong to the same club? How would you dress your staff? What kind of music do you play that makes everyone in one club happy at the same time? What colors and degree of interior finish do you go with in your design? What's cool for the 24 to 40 crowd won't work for the older, more upscale group.

Remember, your target market is defined as 80 percent of your membership and will be in one, two-generational grouping. For example, your target market might be 24 to 40, which means that your club will specialize in this age group and every decision you make as an owner will be with the end goal of attracting more of these people and making the ones you have happy. You may have younger and older members, but your club is designed for that one target market. Consider the following suggested markets and the strengths and weaknesses of each.

Ages 18 to 34. This market is tough to get into because most of the major chains go after this group on a national scale. Clubs built for this market generally go after high volumes and require a lot of sales to keep it going due to the turnover.

Ages 24 to 40. This age range probably doesn't seem much different from the one used for the previous category, but in reality it represents a whole different business plan. Most of the folks in this group are in their second job or beyond, are more stable, and are looking for a high-energy place to workout. This type of club is like a nightclub without the alcohol, although it would be okay to have DJs and free drinks a few times each month if that fits your personality. Clubs with this market fit best in the 12,000 to 25,000 square-foot range.

Ages 25 to 45. This group supports the more rural markets or the family clubs. In small towns, you often have to cater to a wider range of members, but your general target market in these types of locations is going to be a slightly younger overall group due to the presence of so many families. Rent factors often dictate the size of club for these markets, but in most cases lower rents in the rural areas will lead to a decent size club. Clubs as small as 7,500 square feet work can handle the load in the smallest markets, while the family clubs, such as those in the southern states, will often be in the 60,000 to 150,000 square-foot category.

Ages 30 to 50/35 to 55. This emerging group will become even stronger in the coming years. The predicted boomer influx will happen; it's just going to be later than most people think. Boomers that are over 55 didn't really grow up with the fitness boom influence, such as Jim Fixx and the running craze or the advent of Nautilus®

equipment, and not enough of this group will join clubs to make a dent. Those younger than 55, however, are coming to the gym and will do so in bigger numbers in the next few years. At this point, your target market for this type of total-support, upscale facility will be those in the 30 to 50 range, but that will change slowly toward the 35 to 55 age group. These clubs can range in size from 5,000 square feet on the low end to 25,000 square feet. The key is to build a slightly smaller club but to go after the upscale market in your area with higher prices and a higher degree of finish.

You can't be everything to everyone in the fitness business anymore.

Specializations

If you're looking for a narrower niche to fit your particular market or personal interest, consider the following subcategories. Keep in mind that it is easier to compete in a crowded market if you have a unique marketing position. If one of the following types of clubs is lacking in your area, and you have a personal interest in either category, then consider becoming a specialist in one of these growth areas.

Over-50 clubs. Owners who specialize in the fitness-after-50 group can do well in specific markets where the density is high for this age classification. This smaller club would be based upon functional training and lifestyle enhancement.

Sports-performance centers. Few owners have been successful trying to get children to fit into adult fitness. Children don't want to work out on shrunken adult equipment or go through group classes that are nothing more than watered down adult classes done to different music. A booming market, however, is developing in sports performance that fits almost any child. These clubs, developed by pioneers in this area such as Bill Parisi, work to develop the speed, agility, and quickness needed by any child who wants to be more successful in any given sport. Kids of all shapes and sizes do well in this model and units can be built as small as 3,000 square feet up to freestanding models that have adult components in the 15,000 square-foot range.

Mastering One of the Big Three Concepts

The fitness business has slowly been moving toward more specialization and niching over the years. Competition and the cost of building larger units have forced many new owners to go after narrower niches in their marketplaces.

When you start to piece together that ideal club in your head, keep in mind that many of the old-school clubs offered almost everything but really did few things well. These clubs might have had group classes, but they were offered in one, plain room. They might have also had training, but rented out to outside trainers instead of building an internal program. These clubs felt compelled to offer almost anything someone might ask for in a membership, but because the club owner didn't really specialize in anything, most of the offerings were weak or incomplete.

Increased competition, the rise of the more sophisticated consumer, and the increased cost of running a fitness facility have all combined to force the next generation of owners to do fewer things, but to master those that they do decide to offer. The words to remember are "kill the category." Word of mouth comes from offering the ultimate experience for the consumer, and as an owner you simply can't offer this business-changing experience in multiple categories every day in your business.

In other words, what do you want to be known for in your market? If you're going to do something, absolutely kill that category and the business will follow. Master one of the following categories and be competent in the others:

- Group exercise
- Weight management
- Lifestyle enhancement (training)/children's performance training

Think of these categories as the major definers of your business. The one you pick needs to match your market, who you are, what you believe in, and the type of facility you can open due to funds. For example, a Gold's Gym owner in the Atlanta area is so into group exercise that he built a new 20,000-square-foot club with half the space dedicated to five group exercise rooms. He likes group exercise and made it the center focus of his business plan.

Another owner from Texas, on the other hand, built a 27,000-square-foot upscale club but dropped his group program after only six months. His heart was in functional training and he ultimately used the entire facility to meet his needs. The club generated an average of $83,000 a month in training revenue with 3,500 members, but he couldn't make group exercise work at all because his personal interest centered only on training.

Both of these owners are successful in their markets and both built their businesses around their personal strengths. Whatever you do, do it better and with more depth than anyone else in your market and you will have a higher chance of success (Figure 2-4).

Become the Third Stop in Their Daily Lives

Work and then go home. Work and then go home. Work and then go home. At some point, a person wants to get away from bosses, spouses, kids, phones, and the stress of their everyday routine. The clubs of the future should strive to become that spot in the person's life, but owners first have to change how they think about their clubs and, especially, their thoughts about what kind of business they are really in.

What's really neglected in most clubs is the social aspect. The majority of new clubs have everything a person needs to get in shape, but they lack the social heart that makes that club a necessary part of the consumer's life over time.

The important thing to remember is that the consumer's expectations are changing. According to *The Experience Economy: Work is Theater and Every Business a Stage*, by Pine and Gilmore, consumers are raising their expectations regarding what they expect to get for their money. They have moved beyond service as a differentiator and the new consumers will spend more for a great experience.

Most fitness businesses can adequately service the consumer and meet his fitness needs, but few can entertain and delight. Sports bars, stretching areas that serve as socialization zones, cardio theaters, and plush locker rooms are all things that will set you apart in the future from clubs that merely offer fitness.

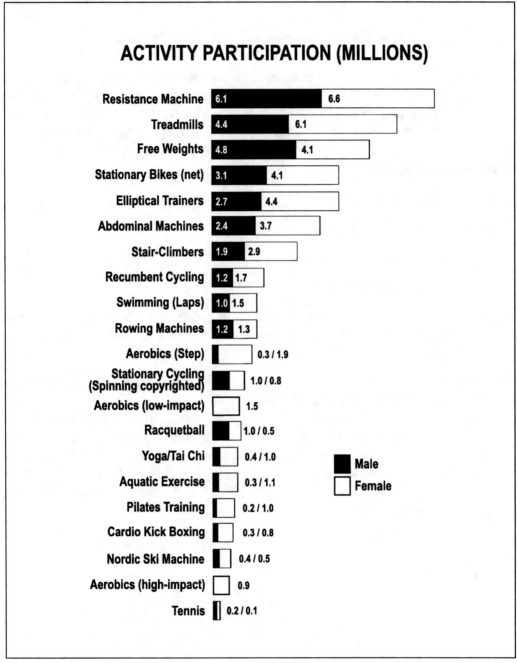

Figure 2-4. Club participation by equipment and group exercise

IHRSA/American Sports Data, Inc., The Health Club Trend Report

Fitness, even at its best, isn't always fun, but no reason exists why your club can't be something that delights the person during every visit and becomes the best part of his day. New owners should remember that the industry is moving beyond fitness and that it is actually in the entertainment business, where every visit becomes an energizing experience that leaves the member wanting more tomorrow.

The Key Concept in This Chapter

Be patient, do your research, look at other clubs and your competitors, and then spend time trying to develop an idea that will help you differentiate your business. Your plan has to match you and your personal interests as well as your market. And remember, master the central focus in your business and kill that category in your marketplace.

Additional Resources

IHRSA Tip: Market Analysis in the Health Club Industry (refer to Chapter 4).

IHRSA/ASD: *The Health Club Trend Report*, 2006

- View key statistics: www.ihrsa.org/research
- Purchase the annual report: www.ihrsastore.com

International Health, Racquet and Sportsclub Association (2006). *IHRSA's Fitness American Style Reports: A Look at How and Why Americans Exercise.* Boston, MA: IHRSA. (www.ihrsastore.com)

McCarthy, J. (2006). *A Progress Report on the Fitness Industry's Plan for Growth: 120 Million Members by 2010.* Boston, MA: IHRSA.
In this book, John McCarthy analyzes the many changes in the fitness marketplace and customer demographics. He benchmarks how the industry is doing in meeting its original 100 Million Member goal. McCarthy also provides insights into how some of the best-run club companies are achieving growth and why he believes that 120 million health-club members, not just 100 million, will exist in 2010 (www.ihrsastore.com).

3

Finding a Home for Your New Business

Once you've conceptualized your new business, you have to find it a home. One of the most frequently asked questions among potential owners considering their first fitness facility is whether to rent, build, or buy a used club. The answer to this question has to match you and your business plan, and will ultimately be determined by how much capital you can raise for your project. Understanding your options with each of these possibilities will help you make a more informed decision and guide you to the choice that will give you the greatest chance of succeeding financially.

Rental Space

When working with rental space, someone else owns the building and you rent that space from the owner for whatever price the market will bear. Your space might be in a strip mall, an office park, or be a freestanding building.

You bring your equipment, finish the interior (called leasehold improvements), and open for business. Each month you pay your rent as well as your share of the property taxes, common area maintenance, and insurance, depending on the amount of space you take in the plaza or building. For example, if you have a third of the space in a strip center, then you would pay a third of the taxes, insurance, and common area maintenance, usually referred to as triple net, for that center.

In many cases, it is much harder to raise money for clubs in rental spaces. As described in Chapter 5, once you put in your lease "hold improvements," such as mirrors and locker rooms, the landlord then owns them if you decide to leave. Even if the landlord let you take down those things, just how much would a used locker room be worth?

This fact makes it harder to raise money from banks or investors for these types of projects, especially if the project becomes larger, because if the owner fails no physical assets are available for the lender to go after that can be sold to pay off the remaining debt. For this reason, owners who go for rental space and borrow money often have to put up a lot more collateral to get started.

Collateral is defined as physical assets that have value that are pledged against the loan. If you would fail, these assets are taken by the bank and sold to recover the money that they loaned you. Examples of assets that bankers like include equity positions in your home, CDs, and stocks, or other property that the bank would have an easy time selling.

Most banks try to get at least 80 collateral against the money you borrow and they expect you to have a certain amount of working capital that you bring to the table. If you have investors who are cosigning for you, they have to pledge assets they own to cover the loan. You may have an investor who believes in you and takes a personal interest in your success, called an angel investor, who might put up the money directly for the project personally and look only for ownership in the business. These types of investors are harder to find, since the return on their investment is often less than they could get for their money if it was placed in more traditional investment opportunities.

Another problem with rental-space financing is that banks that loan money to you will want it paid back in a shorter period of time compared to money used to build. For example, if you need $1.5 million to build a 15,000-square-foot club in rental space, you will probably need to have at least $300,000 (20 percent) out of pocket or as money put up by your investors.

The balance of that money, which is $1.2 million, will have to be paid back in a time period equal to your initial lease period with your landlord. For example, if you have an initial lease of seven years, then the payback time for the bank loan will be seven years maximum:

$1.2 million over 7 years at 8 percent = monthly payment of $18,703

This payback schedule is aggressive and does not include the rent for the facility. But if you found the right property and could get a 10-year initial lease (refer to Chapter 5), then your loan might become more realistic:

$1.2 million over 10 years at 8 percent = monthly payment of $14,559

Just a few extra years makes this business plan look much better, because the payment drops so substantially compared to the seven-year payback. The goal is to free up cash flow that can be used to develop the business during the early years and then reinvest in the business as it ages.

Rental space may be the only option you have, especially in major metro areas where buying a building or building from the ground up is so expensive. If you are opening a smaller club in the 3,000 to 7,500 square-foot range, for example, rental space is often a great choice because you can get in for a lower total cost, and money for a project that size is easier to get from banks.

Once you move into larger projects, the make-or-break part of the deal will come down to the actual rent factor. A general rule of thumb that you can start with that might help you evaluate your ability to do rental space or determine if you need to focus your energies on buying a used club or building from the ground up can be stated as follows. Most business plans, once the club gets bigger than 10,000 square feet, don't work if the gross rent for the facility goes beyond $18 a square foot. An exception exists for every rule, but once the total rent climbs beyond that number in most markets, then the business plan has to become much more aggressive in terms of membership pricing.

Gross rent is defined as the combination of your base rent for the space and your triple nets charges, which are usually billed to you monthly as part of your rent. In this example, once the total number goes beyond $18 a square foot, it's hard to make the plan work in most markets. Your rent is determined as follows:

Square footage x gross rent = annual rent
Annual rent/12 (months) = monthly rent

For example:

12,000 square feet x $18 gross rent = $216,000 annual rent
$216,000/12 = $18,000 monthly rent

This rule doesn't apply in a number of markets. If you are in Manhattan, San Francisco, parts of Las Vegas, or major metro areas in Hawaii, then you couldn't even find a condemned building for $18 a square foot. In those markets, however, you can often get higher monthly payments than you can is most suburban areas, which offset the $18 factor and allows you to break that rule.

Obviously, if you have to pay $28 a square foot for a basement in Manhattan, but can charge $79 per month per member, then your business plan will probably work. But if you pay $36 a foot for boutique space in a suburban mall for a 12,000-square-foot center and only plan to price your memberships at $49 per month, then the business plan will most likely fail, because the rent factor, along with the bank loan, will be more than the business can handle.

Smaller training centers, especially those that add limited memberships, can handle the higher rent factors due to the expected higher return per member. Those type of facilities need to be where the money is and acquiring space in those areas is always more expensive, but is justified by the higher prices you get compared to a mainstream fitness facility.

Building a Club

A lot of the wealth in America has been made in real estate, and when you consider building a fitness facility from the ground up, you are leaving the world of fitness and getting into the crossover world of real estate investment. If your long-term plan is to build a successful business, sell it, and go do something else, in which case how to get out is something you should consider before you actually get in, then building your own building and participating in the real estate side might be your best vehicle.

In this plan, you are actually investing in a building and property and then using the fitness facility, and maybe other rental space in your new building, to pay for that real estate over time. Think of this scenario as buying a rental house and getting a good tenant. You collect rent each month and then use that money to pay your mortgage and keep the place up. Over time, you gain more equity in your rental house as the mortgage is reduced and you might gain appreciation if houses in that area grow in value. If the tenant is a good one and doesn't miss payments, then the investment becomes passive, since you don't have to do much but collect rent, fix some stuff as needed, and sit back and let your investment grow over time.

Owning a fitness business in your own building is very similar. An investor or a bank loans you money to buy dirt and build a new building. Your investor group may own that building as a team and you might have a piece of the building, but you own 100 percent of your club. Keep in mind that two separate companies will be formed in this scenario: one that owns the building and property and another that owns the club.

This practice is done to protect the investors from lawsuits stemming from the club, provide tax advantages for the investment team that owns the property, and keep them free to open other businesses. The simple rule is that most investors, and most bankers through their loans, would rather be in the real estate business than in the gym-owning business, especially if that business fails.

Most investors, and most bankers through their loans, would rather be in the real estate business than in the gym-owning business, especially if that business fails.

A number of advantages exist to building your own building if the market allows:

- It is easier to attract investors who like real estate but don't want to be in the gym business.
- The property serves as the collateral, keeping your cash needs and collateral obligations lower.
- Payback on all loans is much longer, often in the 20- to 25-year range, which results in a much lower monthly payment for the business to handle, thereby freeing up more cash flow.
- Tax advantages related to depreciation, the development of tax trusts, and interest might apply.
- The investors may experience long-term appreciation and wealth-building. At some point, the fitness business might be sold to another owner who then pays rent, or the business might even be closed at some point after serving its purpose of paying down the loan over the years and the building converted into offices or some other use.
- It offers estate planning for those owners who wish to provide wealth for their families in the future.

A number of advantages exist to building your own building if the market allows.

Most fitness facilities require a minimum amount of land, which is also a consideration for your market. Local codes also add to your land needs, especially in areas such as parking and retention ponds. Your minimum needs, however, will be an acre and a half for almost any type of facility and can go up to 10 to 12 acres if you are considering a tennis facility or a large, multipurpose family complex.

One of the current trends in club design and building is to acquire land on prime streets and then build a retail center on the first floor and place the club upstairs or toward the back of the plaza so that it is surrounded by other retail space closer to the street and is in a more desirable location for commercial retail. This type of space has not been open to fitness owners in recent years because of the cost of buying prime lots on the best roads in your market. The cost of the land itself in many suburban markets has risen so dramatically that a typical business plan for a center that has main street frontage won't work.

Developing a building that offers prime retail space at street level, though, allows the club owner to build his center upstairs in secondary space, offset the cost of the gym's rent by making a profit on the retail space, and still have the advantage of having his club visible on a main thoroughfare. Investors are again more likely to want to put money into a project that has multiple sources of revenue that further offsets the risk of just being dependent on the club itself to pay all of the rent. This type of venture, featuring the combination of retail space and a working club, provides more attractive bait to get your investors involved.

An important thing to learn at this point is that a fitness business is a destination business, which means that the consumer will leave his house and head directly to the club as the main stop. This same consumer will also support all the businesses that surround the fitness facility rather than drive all over town running errands. This point should come up often with your investors and bankers.

All of the small businesses that are located next to a fitness center usually thrive because they live off the constant traffic that a club generates day after day. Landlords often like to have a fitness center in smaller plazas because the other tenants are more likely to stay in business and pay rent longer to the owner. The term for this type of business is an anchor tenant. When you present your plan to investors and bankers, knowing the role the club plays in relationship to other businesses in the area, especially if those businesses also rent from your partnership, is important.

Buying a Used Club

Used clubs aren't glamorous, which is probably why most people don't consider buying them when they are first trying to get into business. An emotional element is also in play. New owners, especially those who have not yet been in the business, often believe that their new gym, designed their way and with their ideas, will draw thousands of members (a variation on the famous line from *Field of Dreams*: "Build it and they will come.")

Any small business is difficult and fitness businesses aren't any different. You will have staff issues, marketing challenges, competition that is aggressive, and a number of other factors that make rising to the top possible, but not always easy. Your ideas of service and how you will train people are important, but the bottom line concern is as follows: Does your business plan make sense financially and can you get enough money to open your new club?

Used clubs can often help a new owner get into business with a lot less money, since the outgoing owner might be willing to finance you in and himself out. For example, an owner who has been in business for a number of years might want out and might be willing to let you buy the business with about 20 percent down and then carry the note himself for five to seven years. Selling a business takes time and a seller in a hurry might want to carry the note to get it done quickly. The problem with used clubs is that the current owner often wants more for the club than it is worth.

The used club's listed sale price is often based upon components such as repaying parents, paying off some debt, and getting enough money together to start again doing something else—and maybe buying a new car. Offerings (the listing sheet the realtor or club owner will provide defining the price and what it includes) for used clubs are seldom actually based upon what the club might really be worth but at least provide a starting point for your negotiations.

Before buying a used facility, have your attorney send out a letter in your desired market to all existing clubs. This letter should state that he represents an experienced investor looking for a fitness business and/or the property for sale. All responses should be sent to his office and you should not be listed by name. You may get a handful of responses and most will be high dollar, as everyone dreams of finding a naïve person willing to overpay for a business. Ignore the price at this point and just try to find out who might be interested in selling. Obviously, you should only do this if you are seriously interested in buying a club in that market.

You can also contact local business brokers for any listings in the area for clubs. The broker may know of a business that is for sale but not listed formally. Many owners are willing to sell but don't want to let anyone know because rumors of a club for sale might stop future membership sales if anyone thinks the club is in trouble.

If you get any interest, you need to take the next step and get an offering sheet from the owner, which lists the price and what's included. Don't get too concerned about the price being too high, which is to be expected. Your next step is to sign a confidentiality agreement that protects the seller. These agreements in theory keep you from getting all his numbers and then opening across the street from him because you know he is weak.

Once you get access to his financial information, you can do your research and then make an offer based upon what the business is really worth and the desired financing. The business' approximate value is based upon this formula:

Business value = (EBITDA + owner's compensation) x (3–5) – debt

EBITDA stands for earnings before interest, taxes, depreciation, and amortization. This value looks scary, but all it means is, how much did the owner make in profit before he incurred interest expense, paid taxes, took his depreciation allowance, and adjusted for amortization? EBIT, in other words, is your pretax net before you get taxed. Depreciation is a noncash expense that shows up on the statements, making the earnings look less than they really are because you will actually have that money to use when you buy that business. Amortization can be defined as things such as the money you pay up front to buy a franchise as intellectual property.

You must also add back the owner's compensation, because once that owner is gone, whatever he took out each month stays for you to use. Owner's compensation goes beyond salary and can include cell phones, health insurance, travel expense, car payments and expenses, and anything else he runs through his business. Do not, however, make any adjustments if the owner tells you he is taking out actual cash each month. You cannot verify that number, nor should you try. Taking cash directly out lowers the value of the business and is a bad business move when it comes to the IRS as well.

Once you come up with a total number using the information provided in this section, you then need to apply a multiplier. Multiplying earnings is a way to determine how many years it would take to pay back the purchase price. For example, if you had an EBITDA/owner's compensation number of $150,000 and multiplied by three, then the business would be worth about $450,000. In other words, it would take you three years at the current earnings rate of $150,000 to pay for your business.

Every type of business has a multiplier attached to it, but most are offered in ranges rather than actual set numbers. Restaurants, for example, often have a multiplier range of four to eight. Picking the right number is the art form of business pricing, but can be made it easier when it comes to buying a club.

Many sellers list their club in the seven to eight range because a few of the big-name club groups have sold for that during recent years. The buyers for those groups, however, weren't just buying clubs; they were buying a concept that they felt could be turned into a national, or even international, brand. For example, how much would Starbucks have been worth if you bought the entire company when it only had 20 units? Would you buy the profits of just 20 stores or would you pay much more for an idea that could be turned into 10,000 units?

Independent clubs usually sell in the three to five range when it comes down to the actual sale. If you're buying, you start at two, and if you're selling, you start at seven to eight and get talked down. Where you get into trouble is paying more than the club is worth because you have no reference point in your negotiations.

Think of three as being for a club that has worn lease holds, dated equipment, and needs a lot of work to be turned around. Think of five as being for a club that you could walk into tomorrow and start making money without having to change a whole lot. The more you have to invest initially, the lower you want to offer.

Buying a Club That Is Losing Money

If no earnings exist, then you are just buying the assets of the business. Cash flow may be present, however, and that still has value as an asset of the business. For example, a club owner might be losing money monthly but still have a monthly check from his member payments (net receivable check) of approximately $20,000.

You can approach this business in several ways to get a working value for your offer. First, you can multiply the net-receivable check times 12 (12 months). In this example, $20,000 times 12 months is $240,000. This working number is a rough idea of what this business might really be worth. This number would include all equipment

Every type of business has a multiplier attached to it, but most are offered in ranges rather than actual set numbers.

and deduct the debt of the business. In other words, if the seller owes $100,000, then this debt would have to be paid off as part of the purchase price.

For example, an owner is offering a 12,000-square-foot club for $400,000. The club's expenses are $60,000 and the owner is depositing about $55,000 per month. He isn't getting killed, but his ship is leaking slowly. He floats the business by catching up once in awhile during a good month, skips his salary because his wife has a job, or runs a consistent 30 to 60 days behind on his bills. The equipment is at least five years old, the club needs repairs, and the owner is motivated to sell. He does, however, have a net check from his members of $20,000 per month. What is this club really worth, since it isn't profitable but it does have a few assets?

The working value listed is a solid reference point to get started. All you are buying in this case is the cash flow from the members and some used equipment that needs updating (five years is the max point for most equipment, especially cardio) and the $240,000 figure is probably close to what this business is really worth, though an emotional seller may not let go of his business for this number.

You are looking for three things for when it comes to asset purchase that might increase the value of this business. First of all, do you have the right to perpetuate the business with the lease and at what price? Businesses that have leases due to expire soon and without fixed options aren't worth much, if anything at all. Don't buy the club unless you have a letter signed by the landlord giving you the right to take over the lease or stating the terms of your new lease. If the lease has solid options, and is below the market value, then this business is worth more because it would be hard to duplicate this space at this price.

Secondly, how much is the draft from member payments and can you verify the $20,000 in this example? Don't take anyone's word for what they are drafting each month from current members and don't believe the financial statements without verifying this number for yourself.

If you can't verify that number, then walk away, especially if the owner is collecting his own memberships, which leaves room for a lot of misleading on his part. This receivable base, or cash flow, from member payments is worth more if a reputable, third-party financial service company, is collecting the money. Consult the International IHRSA associate member directory for a complete listing of these companies.

The third issue concerns equipment and what is usable in the club. Owners in trouble list their used equipment too high. Shop the vendors and find out how much it would cost to completely outfit the club with new equipment and then compare that number with what you are being asked to pay for the used stuff. If the owner in this example took care of his equipment, and you could get another year out of it without having to replace everything, the club might have more value beyond the quick reference number of $240,000.

If no cash flow exists to speak of, meaning that the owner has cashed out most of the members or doesn't have many paying monthly, then the sale becomes nothing but a hard asset sale, which creates the following question: What is the liquidation value of this business?

In this example, if his monthly receivable check was only a few thousand dollars, or the actual amount each month was hard to verify, then you would ignore this factor and make an offer for the used equipment (most used equipment with this age might be worth about 20 percent on the dollar of what he paid for it), the right to take over the lease, and whatever else he might be selling, such as desks and computers, which aren't really worth much used. In extreme cases, you might just assume the debt; get the owner out of the lease with the landlord and he walks away.

Other Hints for Buying a Used Business

Get a realtor involved and find out if any new clubs are coming into the market that the seller is not telling you about. Also, check with the city and see if anything is changing with the road or access to the club. One owner bought a club and then found out that all the traffic was being diverted for two years to another road while the city widened the current street, effectively putting him out of business.

Check and see if the loans and leases are assumable. You can often just take over the bills of the failing owner and he will walk, but first find out exactly what is owned and if it can be assumed. The ideal situation is for you to take over payments but leave everything in the old owner's name.

You seldom buy the seller's corporation, because you would then assume all future issues, such as lawsuits. Get an accountant and attorney involved in this from the start and get professional help to value it and make sure you are missing nothing.

Real estate is always handled separately. Avoid lumping the business and property together and get prices on each. Lumping the two will cloud your judgment and often lead to paying more than the individual parts are worth. Real estate is usually valued by using local appraisers, but the bad news is that if it is an older property, such as an old racquet facility, some appraisers value low because they consider the building single-use and, therefore, of little value on the open market unless another gym person buys it. If you are seeking bank financing, your banker might insist on using the bank's appraiser, which again might work against you by lowering the value. Gap financing, meaning that the seller gives you a note he holds for the difference between what he wants and what the bank will finance, may be an option if you, and your appraiser and real estate expert, think the building might be of higher value over time than the bank will lend initially.

Another issue with property is that in hot real estate markets, the building might be worth more money, which forces a higher mortgage than the business can support. In other words, it may be a great business with great cash flow and still not be able to carry a note for the building, which is worth more torn down or converted into retail space than it would be as a fitness business. Get a local real estate expert involved if real estate is part of the deal. You will also probably need a strong real estate attorney as well. Also, make sure the real estate agent is working for you. If he is the listing agent, he might be nice and supportive, but he really works for the seller, which is not in your best interests. Get your own expert and make sure he works for you.

Terms are everything. Try and buy with as little as 10 percent down and payments over five to seven years, if possible. More sophisticated sellers will want at least 20 percent down, but the length of the note can stay in the five-to-seven-year range. The business might be worth more if you can get favorable terms, such as a low down payment or a balloon later when the business is healthy.

Before you buy, insist on a 30-day discovery period, which gives you time to tear into all the financial records of the business. Don't put a lot of value on the statements, since they are easy to adjust to make the business look better. If you are buying a single unit, go in and reconstruct the business from the checkbook and bank statements and find out what the seller is really paying to run the place. Bank statements are also worth in-depth study. Sellers will sometimes pad their business before selling by re-depositing money over and over again, which looks good on the statements but will be obvious when you go through the bank statements. List all the vendors, define who gets what, and look for any unusual transactions with the deposits.

One important thing to remember about buying a used business is that if a club has members and has been in business for a few years, something is right about that location. Starting new clubs is more exciting, but the day you open you start with zero members as compared to buying a used club and walking in with members in place and with money already coming in each day.

Many used clubs aren't worth buying because of the price, location, or how they were built. A few, however, exist in almost every area that are worth considering if they can be bought for the right price and with the right terms. Do your homework and get a proper value on the business before you make an offer. Don't get emotional and be prepared to walk away if the seller simply won't come off a bad price.

One final point about buying used is that while it might not be glamorous, it often saves money and lowers risk. The seller may not be a great operator, but if he has been in business at that location for a number of years and has members, then he has validated the site. Buying an older business that needs fixing up but has 1000 members is often much more cost effective then building a new business that opens with no members. Unfortunately, most start-up people can't get past the excitement of having something shiny and new to play with that was built with their own hands.

The Key Concept in This Chapter

All three options—renting, building, and buying used—have their strengths and weaknesses. Your choice has to fit the market, your budget, and your ability to raise money.

Don't be afraid to start at a lower level. If you can't get a plan together to open that dream 25,000-square-foot club, then maybe buy a used 10,000-square-foot place already in business. If that is too much, maybe open a smaller hybrid-training center that will at least allow you to get into the game.

Additional Resources

McCarthy, J. (2004). *IHRSA's Guide to The Health Club Industry for Lenders & Investors* (2nd ed.). Boston, MA: IHRSA.
This unique reference will be especially valuable to club owners who want to educate their current investors, or who are seeking new investors or refinancing. www.ihrsastore.com

IHRSA Tip Sheet: Selling Your Health Club
Thinking of selling your club?
This IHRSA tip gives 10 essential steps to a successful sale.
http://www.ihrsa.org/tips

4

Finding the Proper Site for Your New Business

What makes the right site for a fitness business and would you recognize a good one if you saw it? Do you look at freestanding buildings or could you make it with a mall or strip plaza location? Is it worth the risk to take a reduced rent but be in the back of an industrial park? Do you just goes for it and throw all of your money into a prime location on the best corner of the best street in town?

A number of additional factors have to be considered before you make your final site selection. Any one of these factors is worth noting alone, but where the magic comes in is understanding how all of these factors combine to influence the final success of your new business.

For example, you might find a great site in a plaza that has Wal-Mart® anchored at the other end. You have great parking, traffic through the plaza all day long, and it looks great for a club, but after three months of negotiation, you find that Wal-Mart has restrictions in their lease that prevent fitness centers from being in the same mall. Why didn't anyone tell you up front? Because it's your job to ask the hard questions going in and to keep your project on track.

In another example, you find a site that has great visibility from the road and has great drive-by traffic, but the city has very strict sign codes that prevent you from signing your location properly. Signage is a key factor that can make or break a location and is something that has to be on your checklist for every site you consider.

As you review the factors covered in this chapter, look at how each one affects the others. A good site for a new fitness business would have the strongest combination of all factors.

Demographics of the Area

Everyone throws around the word demographics, but not too many people understand what the word means and how it affects the process of finding a fitness location. Some new owners, for example, only look at the shear number of people in an area. In northern New Jersey, you might have more than 200,000 people living within three to five miles of your club, but just a few hours away and you're in eastern Pennsylvania in a town of only 20,000 people. The key factor for these two sites isn't the volume, but the rent factor and the concept you are trying to squeeze into the market.

A number of ways are available to get demographic information about your new area. First of all, if you're working with a realtor, he or she should be able to get you current information about your location. Most realtors subscribe to a number of companies that furnish demographic information and should be able to get you info on your site at no cost. Most of the marketing companies that specialize in the fitness industry, such as Ferret Brothers Marketing or Susan K. Bailey, usually furnish carrier route radius reports for free and are good starting points for most site analysis.

What are these tools and how do you use them?

Demographic reports, such as those furnished by a realtor, usually provide information about the people who live near your proposed site. To get this information, you submit your targeted street address and then the information is pulled off the computer for people within a certain distance of your site. Ask for one-mile, three-mile, and five-mile rings when you gather your first information. If you are in a rural area, extend your search to seven miles from the proposed site.

This type of report will tell you how many people are in the area, broken down by ages and distances from the site. Other information, such as household income, race, average house price, and number of kids, is also included.

Carrier route radius reports go after the numbers from a different angle. These reports give you a total of all the mailing addresses by zip code/carrier routes, starting with the site's address and moving out away from the club by distance. This report also gives you the number of multifamily homes, single-family homes, running total for all households in your market, household income, and age information if you desire it. If you use this report, ask for rural route addresses and P.O. boxes as well, since they are not always part of the standard package (see Figure 4-1 on next page).

Carrier route reports usually don't list the total number of people, but rather the total of households, with mailing addresses. You may estimate the number of people by taking the combined total at any distance and multiplying it by 2.2 people per household, which gives you a working number.

Much of the information in these reports may seem confusing at first, but you can focus on just a few things, including the following:

- Household income
- Multi- vs. single-family homes
- Ages

The higher the household income, the more likely someone is to join a club. It is generally recommended that you concentrate on trying to market to the top 60 percent of the people in your area as designated by their household income. If you are going for the upscale market, then focus on the top 40 to 50 percent in your area. Focusing in this way is simpler than it sounds. If you are using the carrier route radius report, run the entire area once to see what's there and then rerun dropping the lowest 30 percent by household income. The marginal 10 percent is good to reach out to occasionally, or if you are operating a family facility.

Household income is situational for your area. If you live in a rural market in a southern state, the top household incomes on your report might be $60,000, which

Silverton Fitness Carrier Route Report

Zip	Route	City	Home	Apt	Total	Income	Med_HV	Age	%Child	Distance	Accum
97381	C002	SILVERTON	391	64	455	49873	146394	52	28	1 min	455
97381	C001	SILVERTON	411	51	462	62954	156538	54	29	1 min	917
97381	R005	SILVERTON	421	202	623	49141	164151	60	22	2 min	1540
97381	R006	SILVERTON	273	52	325	71861	153947	57	26	2 min	1865
97381	C003	SILVERTON	581	110	691	57456	147126	52	40	3 min	2556
97381	R004	SILVERTON	636	144	780	61410	166667	58	23	3 min	3336
97362	R002	MOUNT ANGEL	354	231	585	59266	131731	57	33	8 min	3921
97381	R002	SILVERTON	385	24	409	75606	183333	55	24	10 min	4330
97362	R001	MOUNT ANGEL	342	130	472	48630	128125	50	36	14 min	4802
97381	R001	SILVERTON	449	4	453	94390	215541	56	22	15 min	5255
97381	R003	SILVERTON	404	6	410	78510	204630	59	23	17 min	5665
97305	R002	SALEM	392	0	392	78888	171528	57	28	17 min	6057
97305	C037	SALEM	590	46	636	63000	137879	57	26	17 min	6693
97303	C038	SALEM	591	100	691	64103	128020	48	37	19 min	7384
97305	C045	SALEM	803	0	803	81558	138830	47	38	20 min	8187
97305	C017	SALEM	522	250	772	30878	135638	67	16	20 min	8959
97303	C026	SALEM	533	46	579	46394	115144	50	30	20 min	9538
97305	R006	SALEM	437	41	478	57815	160185	63	19	21 min	10016
97305	C050	SALEM	695	0	695	43786	114798	46	39	21 min	10711
97305	C003	SALEM	762	15	777	58628	121250	59	20	21 min	11488
97305	C041	SALEM	654	421	1075	32971	115599	53	23	21 min	12563
97301	C066	SALEM	635	367	1002	19669	N/A	47	25	21 min	13565
97301	C076	SALEM	51	196	247	29792	N/A	46	15	21 min	13812
97301	C064	SALEM	387	33	420	29653	N/A	51	19	21 min	14232
97301	C075	SALEM	22	0	22	31875	N/A	45	34	21 min	14254
97303	C009	SALEM	718	100	818	38720	116981	50	35	21 min	15072
97303	C028	SALEM	753	190	943	24755	110489	53	24	21 min	16015
97303	C021	SALEM	393	247	640	30339	112500	50	28	21 min	16655
97381	H062	SILVERTON	277	9	286	79156	214063	53	30	22 min	16941
97071	R002	WOODBURN	397	0	397	78727	217361	53	33	22 min	17338
97317	C012	SALEM	461	2	463	80956	N/A	55	22	22 min	17801
97305	C027	SALEM	742	30	772	77153	132197	58	19	22 min	18573
97305	C031	SALEM	684	142	826	60733	121853	54	22	22 min	19399
97305	C025	SALEM	701	143	844	27048	117518	52	30	22 min	20243
97305	C035	SALEM	594	470	1064	53785	138007	53	24	22 min	21307
97071	C002	WOODBURN	695	128	823	45459	133519	49	28	22 min	22130
97301	C021	SALEM	747	125	872	59152	113205	53	29	22 min	23002
97301	C069	SALEM	372	182	554	27852	N/A	50	29	22 min	23556
97303	C010	SALEM	591	94	685	50525	120536	57	23	22 min	24241
97301	C067	SALEM	470	25	495	28750	N/A	48	27	22 min	24736
97303	C040	SALEM	532	143	675	59120	121058	51	24	22 min	25411
97301	C068	SALEM	355	227	582	29653	N/A	48	22	22 min	25993
97305	C043	SALEM	786	513	1299	38265	121318	51	27	23 min	27292
97301	C015	SALEM	678	286	964	39502	114274	53	24	23 min	28256
97301	C032	SALEM	391	496	887	30745	112500	57	23	23 min	29143
97301	C019	SALEM	179	165	344	56261	117672	66	11	23 min	29487
97305	C002	SALEM	376	812	1188	21081	106667	42	28	23 min	30675
97301	C072	SALEM	712	31	743	40870	N/A	51	26	23 min	31418
97303	C042	SALEM	703	0	703	96554	141880	51	29	23 min	32121
97301	C061	SALEM	629	74	703	27695	N/A	50	19	23 min	32824
97301	C063	SALEM	537	61	598	33257	N/A	49	25	23 min	33422
97303	C011	SALEM	547	2	549	61987	121824	56	26	23 min	33971
97301	C073	SALEM	433	16	449	24152	N/A	48	21	23 min	34420
97026	R002	GERVAIS	286	4	290	54336	123750	45	34	24 min	34710
97038	R003	MOLALLA	457	0	457	66613	225000	56	25	24 min	35167
97305	C029	SALEM	951	0	951	44568	123818	50	31	24 min	36118
97305	C005	SALEM	462	0	462	60499	128956	59	23	24 min	36580
97071	C012	WOODBURN	402	250	652	34607	127907	55	24	24 min	37232
97303	C012	SALEM	599	474	1073	62273	161520	54	22	24 min	38305
97301	C070	SALEM	443	2	445	47366	N/A	52	20	24 min	38750
97071	R003	WOODBURN	286	134	420	56108	155625	53	23	25 min	39170
97305	R018	SALEM	90	0	90	74209	162500	51	23	25 min	39260
97071	C004	WOODBURN	458	31	489	50409	130970	53	35	25 min	39749
97305	C033	SALEM	251	0	251	26636	113095	56	18	25 min	40000
		Grand Total	31859	8141	40000						

Figure 4-1. Carrier route radius report

represents a lot of buying power in that type of market. In Connecticut, on the other hand, $60,000 might not even make the top 60 percent in certain areas. It's all relative to your area, but the main factor stays the same: Those with the most money in your area are more likely to join a fitness facility and are the folks you should be going after with your business plan.

In a perfect fitness world, you would want a ratio of two-thirds multifamily homes and one-third single-family homes. In this scenario, you gain the turnover from the condos and townhouses but also have a certain degree of stability from the single-family residences. In most areas, multifamily units, especially apartments, turn over at about a 33 percent rate per year, while single-family homes only turn over approximately once every seven years. Density is also an issue with single-family homes in the nicer neighborhoods. A lot of money may reside in a subdivision, but only 250 homes may be scattered across a very big area.

The aging trend of your area is important if you are going to specialize in the upscale market or if you're looking for kids. This number is more readily available on a standard demographic report. The area's population is usually broken down into categories, such as 25 to 34 and 35 to 44. If you were trying to build a club based on the 30 to 50 group, you would simply look at the total percentages those ages represent in relationship to the rest of the population. You should also include the group just below and the two groups above your market in most cases. Remember, your target market represents approximately 80 percent of your membership and that likes attract likes. Groups that are a little younger or just slightly older than your target market are potential members as well.

You can find research showing that the higher the average household income, the more likely someone is to join a health club. *IHRSA's Guide to the Health Club Industry for Lenders and Investors*, by John McCarthy, is a must-have book when you submit your business plan to the banks or to your investors. This book lists research from American Sports Data citing that those folks with household incomes of $50,000 to $74,999 join clubs at the 17.2 per hundred rate, while those people in the over-$100,000 category of household income join clubs at the rate of 24.4 per hundred. Also note that those people in the $25,000 to $49,999 range joined fitness clubs at a rate of 11.7 per hundred.

Another important point to remember is that average income usually matches all the other important factors of the area. Rent, taxes, insurances, wages, and average income all blend together to define an area. Seldom does one of these actors emerge apart from the others, which would force a business owner to drastically adjust the business plan in some unusual way.

For example, a town in the Midwest might have an average income of $35,000. Entry-level employees start at $7 to $8 per hour and the owner expects to open her club with a $39-per-month average price. After looking for several months for space of about 10,000 square feet, however, she narrows her choice to a spot she likes with a gross rent of $18 per square foot. All the other spaces in town were in the $9 to $12 per square foot range.

This site is unusual in this town and it would have to have some unusual attributes for it to work. Is it an exceptional location with tremendous walk-in potential? Can she build a smaller, more elite facility and use less space, thereby saving build-out cost and rent? Is this boutique space in a very elite part of town that would allow her to charge $49 to $59 per month per member? Since the rent factor doesn't match the rest of her business plan, she would have to alter her business pan to make this site pay off over time.

Another factor in site selection is that the site and finish have to match the average income. San Francisco, for example, has a very high average income—over $70,000 in most parts of the city. But if you pay $36 per month per square foot in rent and then build a typical white-walled, unfinished box gym that you might find in the Midwest or South that reflect a $35 per square foot finish, you won't be competitive in the market and won't last too long.

Visibility

Visibility means that the facility can be seen and instantly recognized for what it is. If a site can be seen easily from the street or intersection, then it has good visibility. If it is easily recognizable as a fitness center because of its front windows or great signage, then the value of that site and the business that location can generate has increased.

Visibility is important because being seen lowers your marketing costs over time. If a site has great visibility from the street, then you are much more likely to get walk-in traffic as opposed to a site that is set at the back of a plaza with no view from the street. Such a location gets little in the way of, "Wow, a new fitness center. I think I'll stop by."

The debate regarding visibility is freestanding building versus strip-mall sites. Freestanding means that the building stands alone, but it does not necessarily mean that the gym is the only business in the building. Strip-mall sites mean that you share a multi-tenant building with other businesses. In this case, you might be one of five different businesses in a strip mall, which simply means one building in either a straight line or L-shape that holds more than one business.

Advantages and disadvantages exist for both types of sites. In a freestanding building, you don't have the advantage of drawing potential members from your business neighbors. An advantage of a freestanding business is that it will usually add to the visibility factor. Freestanding businesses are also often easier to see by a drive-by if they are near the roadway. However, a big negative for most freestanding businesses is lack of parking.

A normal building facility will need about 13 spaces per thousand square feet during its busiest months of the year, which are normally February and March.

Parking

A normal building facility will need about 13 spaces per thousand square feet during its busiest months of the year, which are normally February and March. For example, a 10,000-square-foot building would need 130 parking places during its absolute busiest months. The minimum is 10 per thousand, or 100 spaces in this example, and some city codes go as low as nine per thousand.

Parking is a judgment call if it isn't regulated by code. Most cities, though, have a minimum parking requirement necessary for a fitness-type of business and won't allow you to open if you don't meet that requirement.

In this case, the term "judgment call" has to relate to your anticipated business. For example, a 15,000-square-foot site in Texas was allowed to open with only 80 parking places as a coed fitness center. The city granted the permit, but the club owner suffered because it wasn't enough spaces to meet his members' needs during prime time. This owner sold and the next owner turned it into a women-only club that had parking requirements spread more evenly through the day. The new owner was successful in that location.

You can also help the situation by eliminating as many barriers to open parking as you can. The members, minus barriers such as parking islands, too many curbs, or those old-style concrete barriers at the front of each space, will find their own way and you'll be surprised how creative they can be if you have any open space not lined or limited by hazards. Figure 4-2 cites the average number of parking spaces that clubs that are currently open actually have. Parking can be an issue and you need to make sure your parking meets the business concept you are developing.

Mean	260
Lower 25%	80
Median	155
Upper 25%	270
Data from a sample of IHRSA North American Clubs, 2006	

Figure 4-2. Number of dedicated parking spaces

Know When the Money Arrives

A typical club makes about 65 percent of its total sales between 4:00 and 9:00 p.m., Monday through Thursday nights, and between 8:00 a.m. and 1:00 p.m. on Saturday. These periods are called prime time. They might be an hour later for your club depending on the market. If you own a women-only club, you normally have two prime times, with your first being 8:00 to 11:00 each morning through the week. Again, IHRSA can provide research showing the key hours when clubs perform that can be applied to your business and area (Figure 4-3).

	Open-11:00am	11:01 am-2:00pm	2:01pm-4:30pm	4:31pm-8:30pm	8:31pm-Close
All clubs	33%	15%	12%	34%	7%
Less than 20,000 sq ft	33%	16%	11%	35%	6%
20,000 to 34,999 sq ft	31%	15%	13%	34%	7%
35,000 to 59,999 sq ft	33%	15%	13%	32%	7%
60,000 sq ft or more	35%	13%	13%	32%	7%
Data from a sample of IHRSA North American Health Clubs, 2006					

Figure 4-3. Average percentage of daily member traffic that occurs during various time periods

Knowing your prime time is important because your neighbors in the plaza might influence your site choice. If your neighbors run 9:00 to 5:00 businesses, and you have an after-5:00 prime time, then you pick up a lot more parking when your neighbors close for the day. If you share a plaza with a sports bar, however, or some other late-evening business, then you might have parking problems in the evening since you are both full at the same time. One club owner in Michigan, for example, fought with his landlord for years over the fact that the landlord let a bingo pallor open in the same plaza, which drew hundreds of senior citizens from 4:00 to 7:00 p.m. five nights a week, taking most of the club's parking during its busiest hours.

Signing

The ability to sign a facility is often the key factor for making your final decision about a proposed site. A site with low street visibility, but with a great street sign, can become a strong location and the owner can usually pay less rent for a secondary site.

Signage is one of those things that can make or break a small business, but is often taken for granted.

The problem with signage is that codes vary greatly from city to city, and from mall to mall around the country. The problem occurs when the landlord gives you permission to sign your club, you sign the lease, but the city refuses the sign. Check all signage rules before you sign the final lease and get everything in writing from the landlord as part of your lease.

Signage is one of those things that can make or break a small business, but is often taken for granted. Everyone just assumes that if you own a business and pay rent then you can put up a sign. But if you get lost in the middle of a strip mall and have nothing but a small frontage sign, your business will not do as well as one where the signage is clear and distinct.

Accessibility

A site may have a great sign, nice visibility, tons of nice cars whipping by on the main road just in front of the club, but the location still might not work if the site is not accessible. Accessibility refers to how easy is it to get to the location once you've seen it. You might have strong visibility from the main road, but if you have to drive several miles to the next exit and then take a frontage road to the location, then your walk-in traffic will suffer accordingly.

The rules are simple: Can the consumer pull into your location from several different points? Is the club on a road that has a central island that prevents someone in the opposite lane from turning directly into your center?

Test your potential accessibility by trying to get into the center from several different angles during prime traffic hours. If you get frustrated or have a hard time, then your members will too, and your potential members may not even stop.

One final point is being on the correct side of road during the right time of day. Most clubs have more traffic after work, so you might want to consider being on the going-home side of the road. For example, assume you're standing in front of your site and a steady stream of traffic is in front of your club. You'd get excited. You come back at night, however, and all that traffic is on the other side of the road with little access to your location without going through a lot of lights or crossing over at an intersection further up the road.

Other Thoughts

If you aren't from the area, spend more time looking than you might otherwise, and consider moving to that area for a few months before you make your final decision. What looks good during your first visit may not look so good later when you realize that you are in the wrong part of town. Research the secondary points most new owners miss, such as current and future traffic patterns in front of your business (available from the local department of transportation), get traffic counts for your street, determine if you are on a commuter route, look into any major construction that might be beginning in your area, and most importantly, drive the neighborhoods near your business site until you can't stand it anymore to see how hard or easy it would be for your members to get to you.

If it ain't in writing, then it ain't real—poor English, but good advice. Signs, parking promises by the landlord, agreements with neighbors, and anything else that affects your site has to be in writing as part of your lease or it may not happen. Get it in writing or don't count on it happening.

You also need to look for natural barriers affecting the site. On paper you might have a great location, but things such as train lines, bridges, rivers, industrial parks, bad parts of town, or other concerns affect the people who live there and prevent them from coming to your site. Endlessly drive your location day and night and see if certain natural boundaries exist that might limit membership.

The Key Concept in This Chapter

Location, location, location! Everyone has heard this old adage and it is still relevant today. The second part of this adage that only comes with experience is that failure or success in this business could be determined by being where you are versus being just one block over. Rushing your decision, forcing your business plan into a site because it is the only one on the market, and not getting opinions about the market from real estate experts are all reasons that lead to being in a location that will hurt your business. Take your time and make sure you and your team find the best location you can for your new business.

Good locations are driven by demographics, but the ultimate success of your business will be measured by a combination of factors. When you consider a site, consider everything that might keep a potential member from coming through your door and look for anything that might enhance the location and help you grow over time, such as great parking. Get the location right and the rest of your business plan will be much easier.

Additional Resource

International Health, Racquet and Sportsclub Association (2006). *IHRSA's Profiles of Success*. Boston, MA: IHRSA.
www.ihrsastore.com

IHRSA Tip—Market Analysis in the Health Club Industry

Whether you are considering opening a new health club, buying or expanding an existing club, or overhauling an underperforming facility, conducting a market analysis is the crucial first step in determining whether a need or client base exists for your idea. Nearly all major mistakes in the health club industry can be traced to inadequate market analysis combined with wishful-thinking revenue projections.

Knowing the market's needs and how it is currently serviced can provide you with key information that is essential in developing your business and your marketing plan, including how large to make a facility, what mix of services and amenities to offer, which segments of the market to target, and how much to charge patrons for dues and fees.

If a developer has a preset idea about a facility, the market analysis can test whether the proposed facility would be profitable. In contrast, some market analyses involve a general look at the market, after which the proposed facilities are tailored to suit the market's determined needs.

Avoiding costly mistakes

Begin the market analysis process as early as possible. The earlier you begin, the sooner a decision can be made on a project, which translates into fewer mistakes and less wasted money. An industry consultant can certainly help you six months after your club's opening, but if the business is struggling at that point, it may be due to decisions made before the opening that cannot easily be rectified, such as a poor location.

With a bit of effort, anyone can gather statistics and determine the time it takes to travel to a particular location from any other location. Where a professional comes in is when analyzing the statistics compared to success or failure models. Studying a market is a science. Consultants have a strict set of ratios and rules and will give an objective view of a proposal. Given the dollar amounts involved in even a small-club start-up, the fee involved with hiring a firm for this purpose is probably a wise investment.

A developer can expect to spend from $5,000 to $25,000 for a market analysis by a professional, independent consultant. Generally, for $8,000 to $10,000, you can get a very good idea of what is or isn't going to work, with a fairly high percentage of accuracy.

The process

The predictability of success is based upon parameters set up within the market area. Once the potential location is determined (or chosen arbitrarily, if need be), professionally compiled demographics are acquired for that location. Note that the address should be exact (e.g., the corner of Maple Ave. and 5th Street), as statistics from one quarter-mile away won't necessarily provide accurate results. Several census-type analysis companies can provide this data.

Location, location, location

Needless to say, where you locate your facility is perhaps the most important decision you will make as a developer. The health club industry is a market-driven business. When the decision to join is being made, customers want to know that the site will be convenient for them to travel to several times each week.

During a market analysis, the isochrone (or critical time trade area) is isolated. The isochrone is defined by the time it will take people to travel from their starting location to the club. A market analyst will go to the exact location and travel via automobile, foot, public transportation, or however people who would patronize the facility would be traveling. In the fitness component of health clubs, the isochrone can be divided into two markets: primary and secondary. The primary market is generally defined by a travel time of no more than eight minutes. The secondary market is defined by more than eight, but no more than 12 minutes. A club can expect to get, on average, four times as many members from its primary market than from its secondary market.

Once the isochrone is determined, its demographics are studied. These demographics can include: number of people (residents and workers), occupations (professional, managerial, sales, service, etc.), family household-income levels (as opposed to household income levels, which would include unrelated roommates), orientation (families, single people, businesses, etc.) and education levels. Once this data is gathered, an estimate can be made regarding how many people in the isochrone are likely to join any health club.

Sizing up the competition

Next, a club competitive analysis is done to determine how many competitors exist in the primary and secondary markets (with more weight being given to those in the primary market), how many regular adult users they have (this figure is more useful in a market analysis than a competing facility's number of members), and what segments of the population they serve and how. While a new club (or a club under new management) will likely draw a few members away from other clubs, it is dangerous to assume that a majority of members will be obtained this way. (In fact, in recent years, 48 percent of all new club members have been first-time club members.) It is also worth noting that some people are members of more than one facility at a time. If the market area is overbuilt and the market analysis shows no need for the proposed facility, the recommendation will be against moving forward, at least without modifications to the plans.

Conclusion

It is imperative that someone considering opening, acquiring, expanding, or overhauling a health club ensure—before moving forward—that the facility has the right market position in the right location that matches up with the area's consumer population. If you don't start off that way, it's tough—if not impossible—to fix later on.

IHRSA is grateful to the following individuals for their valuable contributions to this "TIP": Rick Caro, President, Management Vision, Inc. and Dr. Michael Chaet, President/CEO, Club Marketing & Management Services, Inc. Additional information was excerpted from IHRSA's *Guide to the Health Club Industry for Lenders & Investors*, 2nd Edition, by John McCarthy, available at www.ihrsastore.com

5

Understanding Leasing

Trial and error is not the way to learn about getting a lease for your new business. Even if you are using a local professional, which you should, you need to be prepared to guide your team into getting the best lease possible.

The first point when it comes to leases is that everything is negotiable except your name, meaning that you should enter into negotiations with the thought that nothing is firm and almost anything can be discussed before the final documents are drawn. Most landlords, or their agents, expect to deal and normally approach the game prepared to discuss every point if needed.

Being prepared is a must at this stage. Landlords are weighing risk when it comes to renting their space. Can you pay over time or at some point will he have to throw you out, which also means you are behind in your rent and had to be evicted, costing him time, money, and stress?

Know what you want and be prepared to discuss numbers when you get to the actual negotiation point. You can be more casual when you are first gathering information to build a business plan, but when it comes down to making the deal, landlords are much more likely to work with you if you know your numbers, what you want, what you will do to the space, and if you can demonstrate an ability to repay.

Once you analyze a potential site and have narrowed your choices down to just one, you are ready to start the negotiation process. At this point you should have already hooked up with an agent. The most important rule concerning agents is to find out whom the agent is working for in the end. It's common to see a sign, meet a nice, helpful agent, and then start the deal process. The bad news is that the agent on the sign may be working for the landlord and might not be guiding you toward what's best for you and your business.

When you first start looking, it's best to get an agent who represents you and who specializes in commercial real estate. This decision is important, because in small towns many agents do both commercial and residential, but it is always better to find someone who spends most of their time in the commercial world.

You will also need to get an attorney who does commercial leases as well. Find one before you start the process so you won't be hesitant to call and get help with the process as your progress.

Before looking at the basics of a lease, know that you should never break this one important rule: Never start the negotiation without an offering sheet from the landlord or his agent. Offering sheets are usually one-page sheets that list the asking price, size, and other particulars concerning your site of interest. Some agents, knowing that you are a rookie, will not give you a sheet and just tell you to make an offer. Most offers that come this way are higher than what is being asked. Leaving it up to you to start the process is much more desirable for the agent.

Once you get an offering sheet, you may make a counter offer, which is the proper form. Most offering sheets are simple affairs and the real process starts when you lay out your first counter offer, listing everything you want from the landlord, including the rent you submit.

The Basics of the Lease

The ultimate goal is to sign a lease structured to allow your business to grow over a long period of time, and then sell your business to the next person, who will have the right to perpetuate the business into the future. One of the most important elements of any lease is the right to perpetuate the business at that location, at a fair rent, into the future. When you decide to sell your business, a good lease and the right to project the business into the future at a known lease factor, will add a great deal of value to your sale.

Knowing what you want going in makes the negotiation a much easier thing, but you must also think about getting out of your business at some point and selling it to the next person.

Review the following key terms, which you need to know before you get into the lease process. Knowing these terms will help you understand the information being thrown at you, as well as make sure that you don't miss anything of importance.

Base rent. Base rent is the asking price for the space itself and does not include the extra charges you pay for the space, such as your share of the taxes, common area maintenance (CAM), and insurance. When you get your first offering sheet from the agent, the number listed is usually the base rent. The agent/landlord lists that number because it is always smaller than the rent and the other charges combined. Base rent is a part of gross rent, which is the actual number you will pay for your space.

Triple net. Triple net is the combination of taxes, insurance, and CAM. If you are in a strip mall or other type of mall where multiple tenants are present, you will pay your pro-rata share of the combination of these charges incurred by the landlord for the entire property. If you rent a freestanding building, you get to pay all these charges and each bill is usually passed directly to you. If you are in a freestanding building, you can often save money by doing your own exterior maintenance on the property. Beware of the word "CAM." Many agents throw this word around as a synonym for triple net, which is incorrect. CAM refers simply to the maintenance the landlord does to keep the plaza up and open for business, such as snow removal, landscaping, exterior lighting, and lot upkeep, and does not include taxes and insurance for the plaza, which are always extra. Be sure you understand what the agent means and don't hesitate to ask if you are confused.

Triple net charges should be paid monthly along with your rent. Do not go for quarterly fees, because the bills can get really big, especially during snow-removal months in the north. Also, ask for verification of the bills that the landlord incurs. Most landlords will mark the bills up 20 percent before splitting up the charges among the tenants and some fees can be reduced if you question your bills.

Gross rent. Gross rent is the combination of the base rent of the space and triple net charges (Figure 5-1). This number is the actual rent you will pay each month for your space. Consider the following example:

- Your base rent for your space is $10 per square foot (annual basis).
- Your triple net charges (taxes, insurance, and CAM) are $3.50 per square foot.
- Your gross rent would be $13.50 per square foot for the space.

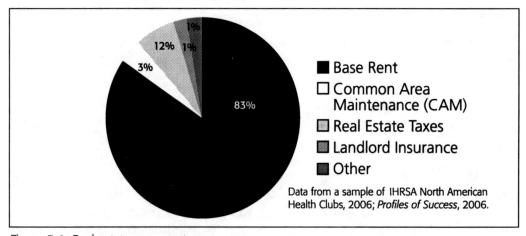

Figure 5-1. Real estate gross rent

Rent can be paid monthly or annually, depending on the region of the country where you live. To find the annual rent, multiply the gross rent per square foot by the square footage. Then divide that number by 12 to find the monthly rent cost as follows:

(square footage) x (gross rent) divided by 12 = your rent payment

For example:

(12,000 square feet) x ($13.50) divided by 12 = $13,500 per month rent

This example is figured on an annual basis. Monthly rents are a little more unusual, but it is good to know how they work as well. For example, an offering sheet might list $0.90 for the space as gross rent. This number represents the amount you would pay per month, not annually. To calculate this number, simply multiply $0.90 by your square footage to find your monthly rent payment. To find your annual rent payment, multiply that product by 12.

For example:

$0.90 x (12,000 square feet) = $10,800 monthly payment

Therefore:

$10,800 x 12 months = $129,600 annual rent

Figure 5-2 shows the annual rent for various types of clubs of several different sizes. The rent shown is broken by per square foot.

Facility Real Estate Rent per Square Foot				
	Mean	**Lower 25%**	**Median**	**Upper 25%**
All clubs	$10.08	$3.97	$6.99	$11.13
Multipurpose clubs	$6.61	$2.37	$4.60	$9.89
Fitness-only clubs	$12.38	$4.90	$8.00	$12.00
Less than 20,000 sq ft	$15.65	$4.67	$8.00	$15.59
20,000 to 34,999 sq ft	$6.88	$3.20	$6.07	$10.71
35,000 to 59,999 sq ft	$6.70	$1.53	$4.02	$12.45
60,000 sq ft or more	$7.92	$3.61	$8.57	$11.04
Data from a sample of IHRSA North American Health Clubs, 2006; *Profiles of Success*, 2006				

Figure 5-2. Facility real estate annual rent per square foot

Vanilla box. Vanilla box is a great term that is often defined on the spot by the person standing in front of you, who usually gives you the version that best supports what he owns and how much he is trying to take you for that day. Vanilla box normally means that your space will delivered to you as a shell with one bathroom (which meets local codes so that the work people can go to the bathroom), a bare concrete floor, cheap lights with an open ceiling, electrical to one box on the wall, and a basic heating and air conditioning unity normally underpowered for your needs while running a fitness center. The walls might be taped drywall, or they might even just be studs.

If you are trying to rent a space that had a previous tenant, you or the landlord will have to do demolition, which means that the space has to be restored to vanilla box prior to you accepting it. The costs related to this process vary, but in most markets it will cost between $2 and $4 per square foot to take it back to the point where you can begin.

It is very important that you get an exact description of what vanilla box means to the landlord because surprises are expensive. One gym owner was taken aback when he assumed possession of his space, after signing the lease, only to find that he didn't have any heating and air conditioning, which was his responsibility to install.

Consumer price index. The Consumer Price Index (CPI) is a government-derived number that indicates how much more money it would take to have the same buying power today compared to the base year of 1967. For example, a year's increase for the CPI might be 1.5 percent, meaning that if a landlord wanted to get the same value for his money, he would have to increase your rent by 1.5 percent. In other words, he needs 1.5 percent more of your money to achieve the same value or buying power. CPI is important in lease negotiations because it is often the universally accepted number used to determine increases in rent, either by the year or during the options periods.

Build-out/tenant improvements. Build-out, or tenant improvements (TI), are what it takes to finish the space, aside from for equipment. This total includes wall coverings, lighting, floor covering, finished plumbing, and locker rooms.

The Lease Itself

The lease itself can be a simple document that is easy to read and understand, or it might be a 100-page nightmare meant to make lawyers everywhere wealthy. The type of lease depends on the property manager or landlord. Most leases, however, are what are called boilerplates, an old term meaning that most of the parts come from software that is used over and over again and cover standard issues common to most leases. A basic lease should contain the components covered in the following sections.

The initial lease period is for five years.

Five years is the standard period of time for your initial lease period and is the period you will most often see on a landlord's offering sheet. You can use the length of the initial period as a tool to barter for something else later in the process.

For example, most landlords take your lease to the banks and leverage its value against other projects he might want to do. Buildings that have space occupied by solid tenants are worth about 40 percent more than a building that is empty when it comes to getting that building financed or borrowing money against a property. Bankers are less likely to loan money against a building that is empty because the owner has to carry the mortgage out of cash flow.

That same building with a proven tenant, meaning a tenant that is paying or has the ability to pay, such as a national tenant in the Starbucks® class, is an asset that might have positive cash flow and is something the bank will lend against or be more willing to finance. The 40 percent number is typical in commercial real estate in most markets but can fluctuate in major metro areas. The individual strength of the landlord and how leveraged he might be in other projects is also a factor.

Using the base period as a tool is simple. Assume that the landlord balks at your request for three five-year option periods. You might counter with an offer to extend your initial lease period to seven years, or even 10 if the space is prime and the terms are favorable, in exchange for getting your options in the future at favorable terms.

Option periods are for five years each and you should normally ask for three five-year options.

Three five-year option periods are becoming obsolete, but it is still a concept worth asking for in your negotiations. These periods give you the right to perpetuate your business, at a known rate, making it easier to budget and worth more when you sell later.

Option periods are based upon CPI and you should ask for a cap of 3 percent.

It is important to have a known rent in the future. Fitness facilities need a constant flow of reinvestment capital to stay competitive, which usually comes from long-term loans from your bank. Without fixed, definable option-period increases, you are stuck with what are called market value options, which means that at the end of your initial period, the landlord can increase your rent to whatever the market will bear.

If it is a hot real estate market, your rent might go from $10 a square foot to $14 overnight. It's hard to build that much of an increase into a fitness business's working business plan. By tying your option period increase to CPI and capping the increase at 3 percent, you can adjust your price increases and capitalization accordingly.

If the landlord balks at CPI, then try for a maximum fixed increase of 2.5 percent per year during the option periods, but if you have to, settle for 3 percent. A fitness business can survive quite well with a fixed increase of 2.5 percent per year or 12.5 percent over every five-year period.

Ask for two months of free rent, including no triple net charges, for build-out time.

It is hard to ask a landlord for five months of free rent. Most agents or property managers are automatically wired to give a traditional three-month period. To break this auto-response habit, you have to bring a different negotiation strategy to the table. Try this strategy, which breaks your desired free-rent period into two distinct areas:

- The first part is a two-month period that allows you to push your build-out along prior to the official opening of your club. Two months is not enough in most cases to do your build-out, but it is reasonable to most landlords. Most landlords are used to building out retail, which is a lot easier than building out a fitness facility. Get your architect involved with sketches and drawings to demonstrate the differences and the time need to complete the project.

- Ask for three months free rent, including no triple net charges, from the date of certificate of occupancy (CO), which is issued by the local permit people and states that you can immediately open for business.

Your new business needs time to get healthy and have a growth phase of its own. Having no rent, or reduced rent, during the first three months to a year allows your new business to get healthy on its own. The perfect combination would be a total of five months with no rent and then reduced rent for the remainder of the first year. This situation, coupled with two months of reserve capital, would make you hard to beat in any market.

Ask for a build-out allowance from the landlord of at least one-third of the build-out costs.

Depending on the strength of your statements, the size of the landlord's pockets, and the time the space has been on the market, you can ask the landlord to participate in the build-out. If your statements are strong, the landlord might put money into the project to get you into the deal, because having a strong tenant increases the value of his property. If your statements aren't as strong, he might put money in but expect you to pay a portion (that can be negotiated) back over the initial lease term.

Even if you are going into the project somewhat weak, many landlords will put some money into the deal that you have to pay back as part of your rent over the initial term of the lease. In any case, ask for at least $15 to $20 per square foot in build-out allowance from the landlord.

Another option might exist if that property has been sitting vacant for a while and the landlord doesn't want to put anything into it. In this case, you might ask for the $15 to $20 per foot, and it the landlord declines, you might counter with the dollar equivalent in free rent during the first year. In other words, the landlord might not want to put money into a project he has been carrying for a long time, but since he is already sitting empty, getting a new tenant might make it easier to fill the rest of the idle space.

Ask for exclusions that limit the landlord from bringing competing businesses into your plaza.

If you are in a plaza or mall, it makes sense to ask the landlord not to take other businesses that might drain away portions of your business. Exclusions are often done as addendums to the lease and your list might include tanning centers, weight-loss clinics, supplement stores, stand-alone juice bars, day spas, and stores that sell fitness equipment.

Always include other fitness businesses in this list. Landlords who are not familiar with the fitness business might not see any harm putting a small, women-only business in a plaza alongside a regular, coed fitness facility.

Ask for the right to sublet space in your own space to other businesses, such as chiropractors, physical therapists, tanning companies, or small insurance offices.

These types of small business pay you rent, thereby reducing your overall rent and helping your business grow through their clients. Some landlords object to this practice, because you can charge more for this smaller space than they are charging you for the club. Therefore, you must make sure you have the right to sublet at your discretion and that the money goes directly to you and not the landlord.

Ask for the right to assign the lease without a lot of legal hassle in case you sell the business to someone else.

You may someday want to sell your business and get out. Most of the boilerplate leases have a very generic clause about the landlord not withholding the option to assign. You want to become stronger by having your attorney draw up a clause that you submit as part of the lease-approval process. If you find a qualified buyer, you will want the right to get out without undue landlord interference.

Ask for the option to buy the property, if applicable, between the second and fifth year.

Even if you are in a strip mall and every dime you have is going into the project, you should still ask. At some point, you will want to own your building. Also, during your journey in small business you might make good money early, find a banker who believes in you, or find that special investor. Think big and always ask for the right to buy the building in the future. Try to establish a predetermined price that will hold during those years

Ask for a clear, written addendum stating your signage rights.

Find out your legal rights to sign your business and get them in writing as part of your lease. Even if the landlord says yes, find out what the city will really let you do and get those rules in writing as well.

Ask for a written understanding of your parking needs.

It is always good to address your parking needs up-front rather than try to deal with the issue when it becomes a problem. Parking is especially an issue if a number of small businesses are open near you later in the evening that might suffer from your parking needs during prime time. Define in writing where your customers can park so that no one is surprised later on.

Ask for a written plan on sound proofing your location if you are in a strip-mall location.

Fitness businesses produce sound that most landlords are not accustomed to with their other tenants and this sound can annoy your neighbors if not addressed before you open. The remedies are easy during the build-out stage but very difficult once the club is open. The landlord should pay for any additional sound insulation that is needed as part of the package, since it affects your business and the ones adjacent to it.

Use rent averaging.

Rent averaging means that you give the landlord what he wants, but you don't necessarily give it to him as he wants it. Your new fitness business will need every advantage it can get during your first year. Averaging reduces your load during the first years but still allows the landlord to get his asking price. For example, a landlord might ask for the following rent during the first five years:

- Year 1: $10
- Year 2: $10.50
- Year 3: $11
- Year 4: $11.50
- Year 5: $12

The average of these five years is $11 per square foot. To give your business an extra edge during the first year, you might offer the following rent structure:

- Year 1: $8.50
- Year 2: $9.50
- Year 3: $10.50
- Year 4: $11.50
- Year 5: $12.50

The average of these five years is $10.50, a little under the average the landlord was seeking, but still within the negotiation range. Most importantly, the landlord gets what he wants, a strong number during the fifth year going into the first option period. You also get what you want, which is reduced rent during your first years that allows your business to get healthy.

Dealing with personal guarantees is a fact of business.

Landlords want you to guarantee everything, especially if you haven't been in business before opening this one. You want, however, the ability to get into other projects in the coming years, which is limited at times by the number of things you are personally guaranteeing you will cover if things go badly. You may offer an addendum that states that you will personally guarantee the lease, but after two years you have a chance to either resign corporately or eliminate the guarantee altogether by stating that if you pay your rent according to schedule, and meet all of your other obligations to the landlord, then the lease can be modified.

Personal guarantees are not to be taken lightly. If you are a new business owner, you will most likely have to guarantee the lease personally. If you are the investor, you most likely will have to sign the lease and guarantee the term, because you are the money person. Understand what you are signing and review the ramifications of this agreement in your state by getting your attorney involved before you sign anything. Some landlords will work with you and let you drop the guarantee if you perform according to the lease. You should always try to include this addendum as part of your negotiations.

Personal guarantees are not to be taken lightly.

The Key Concept in This Chapter

The lease determines your rent factor and is the core item in building your business plan. Understanding how leases work will help you get the best deal you can for your area and business. Find an agent that you like and work with him over the long run. Also, remember that everything is negotiable and that you can go back to the table and retry different deals along the way that will give your business the best chance for success.

6

Steps and Decisions for Your New Business

A number of other decisions will need to be made before you can launch your new business, such as choosing the correct legal entity or deciding if you want to consider a franchise. Begin by first reviewing the steps of opening your business and then address the individual issues separately. These tasks should be done roughly in the order listed, but your attorney and accountant may take you through them in a different order.

The Steps of Opening Your New Business

The following sections present a general checklist. Your local professionals should add to this list as they see fit to protect you from costly mistakes early in the game.

Join IHRSA early and get the developer package.

- Research the industry, and your area, before deciding on the exact nature of your business.
- Attend seminars, such as those offered by IHRSA and the National Fitness Business Alliance, to find out more about what help is available to help you get started.
- Get the info you need to build your business plan, such as the cost of equipment, rent factors, build-out cost, reserve capital, and marketing.
- Don't forget to budget for an attorney and accountant early in the process.
- Visit banks and begin to establish relationships with bankers who work with small businesses. Don't present your anticipated plan, but simply tell them what you are trying to do and find out what they need from you in general. Only give a formal presentation when your business plan is ready and professional.
- Build your business plan and get your money in line for the type of business you plan to open. If you have investors, get their share escrowed or at least get a legal letter of intent before signing leases and legal obligations based upon money being available in the future from someone else.

Hire an accountant and an attorney who understand small businesses and who have set up and advised other small businesses.

- Get advice regarding the best legal entity for you and where you are in your life.
- Start keeping all receipts per your accountant on researching and opening your new business.
- Get tax advice immediately rather than waiting until the end of the tax year.
- Get help on building a professional filing system right away, especially concerning all start-up expenses.

Create the legal form and name of your business.

Make sure to research your chosen business name with your attorney before committing to it. You will also probably choose a name for your corporate structure and then a DBA (doing business as) name for your business. Your business may take one of the following legal forms:

- Sole proprietor
- Partnership/limited partnership
- S corporation
- C corporation
- Limited liability corporation (or company) (LLC)

File the appropriate forms for your state.

- Fill out all legal forms required by your state.
- File your Federal Employee Identification Number (tax ID) and all other tax forms necessary for your city, state, and business type.
- Check to see if any environmental permits need to be filed.
- Complete all city and state filings as needed.
- Be sure to file all city and county permits as required and in a timely fashion.

Consider the following issues with your attorney and accountant.

If you are a corporation of some type:

- Have your attorney prepare your articles of incorporation.
- Have your attorney draft your shareholder documents.
- Prepare your board of director documents with your attorney and accountant.
- Get your minute book, corporate seal, and stock certificates.
- File the proper C or S documents with the IRS.

If you are an LLC:

- Get a partnership agreement in place.
- Determine who will be the managing partner and define that role.
- Determine who will be the limited partners and define their roles.
- Create job descriptions for each partner who will be working in the business.
- Establish who has the right to make the final decision if all partners don't agree.
- File all paperwork with the state and the IRS in a timely fashion.

If you are a partnership:

- File the appropriate tax forms with the state and the IRS.
- Get a rock-solid partnership agreement in place that defines buyout options, what happens in case of divorce or death of a partner, the right to disagree through a third-party arbitrator, and whatever else your attorney needs to do to protect you if your partnership goes bad.

Complete the following general tasks.

- Open bank accounts
- Start getting tax advice for each decision, such as buying versus leasing equipment.
- Work with your accountant if you need to generate any type of early payroll.
- Contact an insurance agent and find out what coverage you might need before you open. Look in the IHRSA resource guide to find an agent who specializes in fitness businesses.

Complete the following tasks pertaining to your first employees.

- Create job descriptions.
- Get some basic human resources (HR) help, including legal hiring practices, legal applications, and interview processes. Again, IHRSA can help.
- Start every employee with a nonsolicitation agreement, which is available to IHRSA members free of charge.
- Get your tax ID.
- Keep secure payroll records.
- Get an employee manual in place before you open.

Legal Entities

Legal entities are important to you for two reasons: the right one provides the maximum legal protection in case you get sued and gives the maximum tax advantages to both you and the partners in your business, if any. The following information is a *brief tour* that describes each entity and explains what it can do for your business. As always, get some professional guidance from a local attorney and tax accountant before making your final decision.

Sole proprietorship

This option is the least sophisticated of all of your choices, both for tax purposes and regarding start-up expense. A sole proprietor is just you, and your spouse if applicable.

Being a sole proprietor means that you conduct business as you and that no other tax entities are in place.

The issue to consider with your attorney is liability. As a sole proprietor, you have total responsibility for all tax issues and legal issues that arise from your business, because all income from your business is passed through to you personally.

A sole proprietorship might, however, be your choice if you want to open a small facility, such as a training studio, without partners and without any very complicated financing in place. Another thing to note about this type of business is that they are sometimes harder to sell because it is harder to determine the assets of the business versus things you own personally. Also, if you die the business usually ceases to exist. But if you only want one, small studio and plan to work it yourself, your discussion with your tax person should begin with a sole proprietorship.

Legal entities are important to you for two reasons: the right one provides the maximum legal protection in case you get sued and gives the maximum tax advantages to both you and the partners in your business, if any.

Partnerships

Partnerships are confusing to most new small-business owners. "Hey," you exclaim at the gym during a set, "You're my friend and workout partner and I want to open new gym, so let's become partners and do it together."

Forming a partnership can be easy. Getting out is always the most difficult part.

First, in a partnership, each partner has unlimited responsibility for all of the business' debts and legal issues. Another way to look at this issue is that once you're in, all the stuff you own personally, such as your house, can be taken to pay for any debt the partnership racks up while in existence.

Blind partnerships, or those that a couple of people form with a little legal help and without a partnership agreement in place, usually fail. Such failure is expensive. Go into your partnership expecting the worst to happen and cover yourself in advance and you will never be disappointed.

The following tips about partnerships should be discussed with your attorney:

- Use your attorney to do the partnership. You will read that you can do this on your own, but get an attorney involved from the beginning.
- Draft a detailed partnership agreement (refer to Chapter 9) and be sure to cover how to end the partnership by buying each other out based upon predetermined formulas.
- Make sure only one person has the right to make the final decision if you disagree. The business has to operate each day and it can't wait for partners to come to an agreement.
- Ask your attorney about selling your interest to someone else. Selling an interest in a partnership is usually difficult because the other partners have to agree to the sale.
- Designate from the outset who has the right to make the decisions when it comes to entering into any type of legal commitments, such as signing a lease for a new printer. Legally, any partner can usually go crazy and sign for stuff, but you should put restrictions on this practice through your partnership agreement.

One final note is that most general partnerships are not based upon percentage of ownership. For example, if you own 80 percent of the partnership and two other people own the rest, you are all equal despite the percentages. Have your attorney explain this issue to you up front.

A subversion of the general partnership, called a limited partnership, requires more stringent legal controls. Again, talk to your professional help before embarking on this voyage. This type of entity does not offer many real advantages, but most new owners and their sidekicks almost always end up discussing a limited partnership when first getting started. Explore this issue carefully, because a limited partnership has many pitfalls and offers little to gain in the long run.

S Corporations and C Corporations

Most people getting into small business will be better off with an S corporation versus going after a traditional C corporation. When a new owner puts together a business, he almost always speaks in terms of the C corporation, which is what you see on many of the old movies about business. The confusion comes when the new owner says, "It's okay, I will own 51 percent of the stock and I will make the decisions."

An S corporation essentially splits the difference between a partnership and a C corporation. The real difference, however, among these entities is the tax aspect, which is the important issue to explore with your tax professional.

With C corporations, the issue of double taxation is always present, meaning that you pay taxes as the corporation on profit made and then you are taxed again when you take any money out personally. S corporations, on the other hand, have different tax rules. In this case, profits and losses are passed through to the owners based upon their pro-rata share of the company. This explanation is simplistic and, again, you need to ask your tax person about the issues and how they affect you and your new business.

Selling an S corporation is also a lot easier than selling a C corporation due to the tax implications of the double taxation. C corporations are an older tool and are not a good choice for most small businesses. They are normally avoided by most people owning a simple fitness business.

C corporations do have one advantage to explore with your team, which is the limitation of liability for the partners. Simply put, if you get sued, the corporation acts as a shield that can prevent the person suing you from going for anything beyond the assets owned by the corporation itself.

A limitation on the liability for debt you are responsible for personally also exists with this type of corporation. If you would have to bankrupt the corporation, for example, the corporate shareholders are not liable for any of the corporation's debts. Landlords and bankers know about this situation, of course, which is why you usually have to sign personally, not corporately, when you enter into a lease or bank loan.

Assuming that you have decent insurance, the protection provided by this entity isn't as important as it used to be. The other entities, if set up correctly by your attorney, can provide a certain degree of protection as well.

A common mistake made by many first-time owners who do property as well is putting the building and the business into the same corporation. Always, without exception, have separate corporations for your property and for your business. Doing so is another way to provide more protection in case you are sued, since your assets are not all lumped together in one company.

Limited Liability Companies (LLC)

The LLC is a relatively new option open to small-business owners and is now legal in all states. The LLC has several advantages worth exploring with your tax person. First of all, the personal liability for the members is limited. Secondly, the tax benefits flow through to the individuals involved in the LLC.

You will need to establish an operating agreement (similar to a partnership agreement) as part of your set-up with this entity. Rules governing this agreement may vary from state-to-state, so make sure you spend time researching them going into the set-up and make sure you do have an operating agreement in place, since most states use a default agreement if you don't establish one yourself. The LLC is the best choice for most small businesses, which is why it should be the starting point of your discussion with your tax professional.

Franchising

Franchising isn't for everyone, but it may be for you. When you buy a franchise, you supposedly buy a proven business system developed by someone who is selling this system to others. To use this system, or franchise, you pay a fee up-front in most cases and then either a flat fee or a percentage each month to the franchisor.

Franchisors usually provide help with site selection, market research, advertising, business training for the owner, staff development, and other business aspects that a new owner would have to develop on his own if he were to open a business without the help of the franchisor. You are also buying the name recognition, national branding, and ability to sell products that are developed through the efforts of the franchise rather than incurring the cost of developing these things for yourself.

The most important rule if you are considering a franchise is to do your homework. Visit a large number of existing units and talk to owners. If you get a negative pattern, walk away and try another option.

Ask the following questions regarding any franchisor with whom you are considering working:

- How long has the franchisor been in business?

- How many units are currently opened (not just territories sold)?
- Is the company growing or stale?
- What kind of reputation does the brand name have in the market?
- It the product unique and defensible over time or would it be easily duplicated by someone else?
- Who owns the franchise and what are their backgrounds? Were they successful in their businesses or just successful in the franchise business?
- Does the franchisor own any company stores and how are they doing?
- Are there any lawsuits pending by franchisees? How many have occurred during the past five years?
- What are the exact franchise fees and how are they determined? What are they used for by the franchise? Does a percentage go toward national marketing or branding?
- Do you have to participate in certain programs each month, such as a national marketing campaign?
- How much training will you get as an owner? How much help can you expect once you open? What kind of help can you get if your business doesn't do well?
- Does the franchise charge extra for onsite visits? Are any other "extra" charges to be expected?
- How do you/can you get out of the franchise if you don't like it?
- What is the failure rate for the existing franchisees?
- How is your territory as a franchisee established? Is it protected?
- Is the length of the initial franchise agreement negotiable?
- What happens if you want to sell your franchise or sell your territory?
- Does it cost more to stay on as a franchise after the initial period?
- What happens if you want to open another different type of fitness business in the same area but with a different name?
- If you die, what happens to the franchise?
- If you are comparing several franchisors, make sure you get down to the actual cost factor per franchise. Some of the cost factors aren't always clear, so make sure you are comparing actual costs across the board.

IHRSA, through its magazine *Club Business International*, publishes a guide each spring listing all of the franchises operating in the fitness business. This guide lists what each one does, along with the number of franchises, contact information, and other facts that will help you begin your investigation, and gives you an overview of how each one fits into the fitness world. Reviewing this list is a great first step, but once you move toward making a decision be sure to get a professional accountant and attorney involved.

Leasing Versus Buying Equipment

Whether to lease or buy equipment is another frequently asked question that comes up early, especially when an individual is considering his first large equipment purchase. Leasing is often a better option for fitness-business owners who have limited capital when they start. For example, if you have decent credit, you can often get a line of equipment for your new club, which can run as high as a half-million dollars or more, for as little as 10 percent down, and sometimes even less. On the other hand, if you purchase $300,000 worth of equipment, it would take $300,000 to place the order. You wouldn't have any monthly payments, but you would need to have a large sum of free cash to get your equipment.

If you leased, you might put 10 percent down, and then have payments for three to five years on the balance of the lease. Your payment for three years at 7 percent interest would be about $8,300 per month, or $5,300 a month over five years. Interest and term could vary, but if you can you should consider leasing your stuff for five years. In this case, your only out-of-pocket expense would be the down payment. You will

Leasing is often a better option for fitness-business owners who have limited capital when they start.

have monthly debt, but you don't have to come up with $300,000 to get your equipment package.

You might also check with your accountant to see if you can deduct your lease payments as a business expense on your taxes. If you can do this, it lowers your net cost of the lease.

Leasing also allows you to deal with the fact that fitness equipment, especially cardio equipment, will wear out in approximately four or five years. It might break down more quickly if you don't maintain it, or it could last longer if you really take care of it, but four to five years is the average, and you will need to replace it somewhere in that timeframe. If you lease, you trade in the old equipment and just pick up a new lease. It is important to remember that if you have gotten that far, your business has been handling the payment anyway and simply extending the lease into the future probably won't be that painful.

Some advantages exist to buying equipment. You own the asset outright and won't have any payments. Some tax advantages are worth exploring with your professional if you are considering buying the equipment under another corporate name and leasing it back to yourself. This option might also be something to explore with an investor as well.

Buying outside your company and leasing back to yourself might also allow you to charge yourself a higher interest rate and payment, thereby letting you take more out of your business. This situation might apply if you have partners who don't want to put the money up for the equipment or if the business is profitable. Again, explore these questions with your tax professional before actually committing to a set path.

You might also be able to negotiate for a much larger discount if you pay for the order up-front. Equipment people are like other businesses that have seasonal highs and lows in that most would welcome a large order paid for all at once and would deal a little to make it happen.

Understanding depreciation

The value of your equipment lessens each year and the equipment will eventually wear out. The name of this process is depreciation, which is a term used by your accountant to write off the value of that asset over time. Another term for this process that you might read about is capital allowances, which is a way of allowing you to write off the cost of capital against the taxable profits of your business.

Before you make any major purchase of any type, consult your accountant to make sure you are covering future tax ramifications before you buy. It is easier to make decisions before you purchase or lease than it is to try and cover your tracks later.

The Key Concept in This Chapter

This chapter is wide-ranging and is devoted to some of the business concerns you need to address as you move forward with your project. As noted, more questions are presented for you to ask your tax and legal professional than specific answers.

How you set up your business and the decisions you make concerning your tax ramifications are more individualized than most people think. How much money you have, if partners are involved, if you already own other businesses or if you plan to open one or 100 additional units, are all questions that can only be answered by you and your professional team.

Study this chapter carefully and share it with your team. If your business is set up by a professional and you begin with the right legal vehicle, you are much more likely to avoid any serious downfalls, such as partner disputes or tax issues, later on when you are making money.

Additional Resources

McCarthy, J. (2004). *IHRSA's Guide to the Health Club Industry for Lenders and Investors* (2nd ed.). Boston, MA: IHRSA.
www.ihrsastore.com

International Health, Racquet and Sportsclub Association (1998). *Uniform System of Accounts for the Health, Racquet, and Sportsclub Industry* (2nd ed.). Boston, MA: IHRSA.
www.ihrsastore.com

IHRSA Tip—Purchasing Fitness Equipment

Each year, the process of obtaining fitness equipment becomes a bit more complicated. New categories, additions to existing lines, more sophisticated features, and new companies all can make the selection of a piece of equipment that much more trying and time-consuming. Obviously, every club has different needs. However, whether you're filling an empty room with new equipment or simply updating your current inventory, you should ask some basic questions when making your purchase.

Questions to ask yourself

What market segments are you targeting? Beyond traditional cardiovascular and resistance-training equipment, lines exist that cater to specialized populations such as women, children, seniors, bodybuilders, and postinjury rehab patients.

What kind of space do you have? Nobody wants to work out on a crowded cardio floor. A general rule of thumb states that 46 square feet of floor space is needed per station. When working with special populations, such as members in wheelchairs, that number may need to be higher.

What are your power constraints? Certain machines, such as treadmills, have large motors and therefore require a lot of power. Some elliptical machines don't have motors, which is a useful feature if adequate power isn't available.

What are your staffing and programming capabilities? Make sure you have (or can hire) the appropriate staff to provide programming for the machines you purchase.

What is your budget? The answer to this question may determine whether you lease or buy, and whether you opt for new or refurbished items. As the level of equipment sophistication increases, so does the cost of buying new.

Questions for vendors

How long have you been in business? New companies may be eager to please and offer attractive pricing incentives, while more established companies may have proven track records and be worth the extra money.

Are you financially stable? You obviously want to avoid buying equipment from a company that is about to go out of business. Imagine trying to get parts or service from a manufacturer that no longer exists!

Are you an IHRSA associate member? All IHRSA associate members pledge to follow the association's code of conduct for ethical business practices.

What's your warranty? Each part of a machine (e.g., frames, belts, chains, upholstery) may be covered under a different warranty, and for a different length of time. Be sure you understand all terms of warranties.

How long is your typical downtime? That is, how long does it take to fix or replace an item that isn't working properly?

How complicated is it to service the equipment? Most manufacturers will train your staff to make routine repairs. Some offer a certified technician-training program and may reimburse you for the hours your maintenance person spends on repairs.

Questions for anyone but the vendor

What's their service record like? To find out what type of service a company really provides, call the clubs on its reference list and ask pointed questions. If you know of other clubs that have the type of equipment you are considering buying, call them too. Ask to speak to the maintenance staff. You want to know what the service will be like after your check clears.

What was the installation like? Did the delivery process go smoothly? Did the manufacturer take care to get the equipment through the doors, around the corners, and up the stairs without gouging walls and tearing the carpet? Was installation as painless as possible for members? Once installed, was the equipment thoroughly tested, and was your staff thoroughly trained on safety, operation, and routine maintenance and repairs?

What do members say about the equipment? Are they getting results? If members find the equipment ugly, intimidating, awkward, confusing, or uncomfortable, it won't be used. Instead, it will serve as a constant reminder that you could have done something more constructive with your money and space.

Considerations by type of equipment

Cardiovascular machines

Desirable features of cardiovascular machine include the following:

- A user-friendly operating display
- Easy-to-read instructions, smooth operation

- Comfort during use
- Well-designed reading/water bottle racks
- Variety of programs
- Heart rate monitors
- Low maintenance

Consider the following desirable features specific to certain types of cardiovascular equipment:

- Bikes should have seats that are comfortable for both women and men, and that adjust easily and smoothly.

- Treadmills should have large and flexible decks, resilient decks and belts, adequate motors, self-lubricating roller bearings, incline and decline features (for balanced workouts), handrails, and automatic program clear (useful in resetting machines between users).

- Stairclimbers should position users to work the gluteus maximus muscles more so than the knees. They should also have large foot pads and a special coating on the handrails that are durable, non-slip, and easy to clean.

- Elliptical machines should allow for a comfortable stance and motion through a variety of stride lengths.

- Rowing machines should provide a smooth rowing motion, with the cable, seat, and flywheel operating smoothly.

Resistance-training equipment

Desirable features of resistance-training equipment include the following:

- Solid frames
- Durable paint
- Sturdy upholstery

Plate-loaded and selectorized machines should contain clear directions and illustrations that are readable to older people even without glasses. Information on these machines should explain which muscles are being exercised and the appropriate ranges of motion. Such equipment should be of biomechanically sound design and should allow for independent movement of the limbs. It should include good grips, be easy to use, and provide negative resistance.

Free weights

Desirable features of free weights include the following:

- Smooth bolt heads on dumbbells
- Rubber-coated plates (which cut down on dings and noise)
- Easy-grip design
- Easy on/off collars

A note about refurbished equipment

Refurbished or remanufactured equipment can sell for between 30 percent and 70 percent of the original manufacturer's price. This discount can translate into incredible savings on what is most often the greatest capital outlay for a facility. Ask vendors for remanufactured equipment if they carry "demo" equipment, which is often like new and may have never been used in a commercial setting.

Conclusion

Remember, you are buying equipment for your members. If they like it, if they can figure it out, and if they can use it safely, then positive results are practically guaranteed.

To search for quality products and services for your facility, visit www.ihrsa.org/buyersmart.

7

Developing a Business Plan

If you want money from a banker or investor, or even an astute family member, you're going to have to write a business plan that clearly and concisely makes your case for borrowing money. You should consider writing two types of plans for your first business project. First, a *prospectus* is the tool you would use with investors and bankers. This tool is usually approximately 15 to 20 pages long and is what a banker is asking for when he or she requests a business plan.

The *development plan* is a tool to help you define your business. This document clearly defines each aspect of your business in detail to ensure that you miss nothing during the project's development and to help you understand all of the components necessary to build this type of business. These plans might be anywhere from 75 to 150 pages in length, and this type of plan is not what a banker wants to see.

The mistake rookie owners often make is that they spend more time building the plan than they do trying to raise money. Writing the perfect 150-page development plan and detailing every nuance, from an anticipated class schedule to the type of amenities in the locker room, is a good exercise in thinking through all the details it takes to create a fitness business, but the last thing a busy banker or investor really wants on his desk is an endless pile of paper representing the smallest details of your proposed business.

Prospectus plans are short and to the point, including such items as a concise overview of the project: who is involved, the cost, a pro forma (a financial projection that shows how the business will perform over a set time, such as two years), and maybe some demographic information. The development plan gets into concepts such as the structure of your group program, people needed per department, 12-month marketing plan, sales training, the tools needed to support the sales department, proposed hours, and other details that help a new owner focus on all aspects of the new business. This plan is for you to create to keep you on track. However, you might be the only person who ever reads it.

Bankers and loan officers are normally serious people who do their best to loan money to people who are prepared for banks and business in general. According to conversations with a number of loan specialists, only four out of 10 people who come in for money have a prospectus/business plan, and out of those four, only one can actually sit down and defend the numbers in his plan. In other words, the person asking for money usually didn't even build his own plan, leaving it to his accountant or a friend to develop it for him.

The Prospectus

The prospectus is a brief history of the universe in 20 pages or less. This universe is the world of your new fitness business, and your prospectus briefly answers all of the major questions in something that can be read in one quick sitting by a busy banker.

The prospectus presented in this chapter was originally based on the Small Business Association (SBA) loan application and has since been modified over the years. This particular model has done quite well with banks and investors and is a proven tool for raising money.

As a side note, the Small Business Administration works with banks to guarantee loans for small businesses. Several types of loans are available through the SBA, such as a 504 designed for an owner who wishes to purchase physical assets including a building, and the 7A loan, designed for owners who aren't buying property.

The heart of every business plan of this type is the projection, which is where you tell the loan officer or investor how the business will perform over time. Solid projections can be constructed for a two-year period, but some lenders occasionally want five-year projections, which are at best very weak attempts to project the business environment too far into the future. If you have a choice, limit the projections to two years.

A prospectus should include the following components:

- Cover page
- Overview of the project/executive summary
- Estimated costs of the proposed gym
- Proposed financing
- Projections and monthly operating expenses
- Bank and investor considerations
- Operating team for the club
- Summary of the project

The prospectus presented in this chapter is designed for an actual club for an existing owner who was seeking SBA or conventional financing. This owner already had partners in place because she had an existing gym, had established a banker relationship that could handle conventional financing as well as SBA loans, and had worked with a realtor to get the real numbers on the property. This plan is the basis of what she used to present to the bank with her final application.

If you are seeking money, find a banker who understands both conventional financing through the bank itself and who can also help you with SBA. If you have experience and a track record, most banks will take your loan through conventional financing, although this decision will vary from bank to bank. You can get further information on the SBA's website (www.sba.gov).

You should also explore Certified Development Companies (CDC), which specialize in helping people package their loans for the SBA. These companies are also a good place to start because their employees have a lot of experience in helping new owners package themselves for banks and for the loan process.

These companies are regional in nature. To find the one nearest you, explore the National Association of Development Companies, which can be found at http://www.nadco.org/.

An explanation of each component of the prospectus is provided, followed by an actual example that includes actual working numbers. All names, including the club, are fictional in this plan, but the plan itself was written to help a young owner get financing for her second club and was actually presented to a bank. This plan was accepted, but the owner eventually changed her goal and acquired another property that had become available nearer to where she wanted to open.

Cover page

The cover page simply gives a quick look at what is inside. It should list the proposed business name, the owners, the date of submission, and contact information for each owner.

Overview of the project/executive summary

The overview section is a one- to two-page overview of the entire project, giving your prospective investors or the loan officer the overall picture of the project. The overview should state what the project is, where it will be located, who will run it, why the area was chosen, and how long it will take from concept to completion.

You might also find that this section is referred to as an executive summary in more formal business-plan templates. The goal is the same no matter what you call it: Give the reader a brief, tightly written picture of your project in just a few pages.

Estimating costs of the proposed gym

The next section is the projected expense section for the entire project. This section would present an overview of the entire project as well as the breakdowns of the individual components. The following components are included in this section:

- Cost of the entire project
- Land costs, if any
- Building costs/the outside shell of the building
- Site preparation
- Build-out for the interior
- Equipment costs

- Reserve capital
- A general category for the miscellaneous items, such as computers, music systems, licenses, etc.
- Marketing costs for the presale period and for the first 90 days of operation
- Architectural fees

Proposed financing

This section should discuss where exactly the money is coming from for the project. You should have an initial idea of where you are seeking financing from and should do initial bank investigation before submitting a prospectus plan to anyone for review.

If partners are involved, their participation should be discussed in this section as well. How the partners will participate financially, how or if they will participate in the day-to-day operations of the gym, and how your partners will be repaid are all items that should be detailed in this section.

Projections and monthly operating expenses

Projections are the heart of the prospectus, because this tool demonstrates the ability to repay the lender or the investor. Most projections should be kept to two years, since the ability to project beyond that becomes somewhat hypothetical and most modern bankers don't have much interest beyond that initial two year-period. In some cases, though, you might be asked to submit a three-year projection. Be aware of several of the common flaws in projections that usually get the loan rejected immediately.

They're not realistic or are too good to be true.

Projections that show no negative cash flow are just too good to be true and the banker knows it from his experience with hundreds of other small businesses. Lenders expect a loss in the beginning and they are more concerned about your ability and awareness to plan for a reserve than to expect no loss at all.

Build a best-case projection, a conservative middle case, and a worst case. Throw the best case away, give the middle case to your banker, and run your club off the worst case. The worst case is important because you want to know how bad it can get and still work.

Don't make the mistake of submitting your best-case numbers. It's nice to dream, but it's safer to submit a conservative set of projections (the conservative middle) to your banker. Experts recommend building the worst case because it is important to know where the bottom is in case something unusual happens during those crucial first months.

For example, one young owner lost several months of prime business because his wife was in a car wreck during the first month he was open. He held the club together, but the strain of taking care of his kids and seeing to his wife disrupted his focus. He made some numbers that were less than he hoped for, but he knew from his worst-case plan that he could still make it. He returned to the business with full focus in about three months and was able to get the business back on track.

You can't defend the numbers.

You're not a numbers person, so you have your accountant build your projections. When questioned, you have no idea where he got those numbers and you sit in front of the banker looking at your own numbers with surprise. This scenario makes bankers nervous and is not going to get you a loan. Be able to defend every line and understand how the money will arrive in your new business. If you can't explain it, you most likely won't be able to make it either.

You have no personal reserves.

If you have to take money out of the business from the first day it is opened, the banker knows that your plan is weak. Show a personal reserve of at least six months to let your business get healthy.

Your projection is not adjusted for the seasons or for the natural flow in the business.

A straight-line projection might be one of the most common mistakes a new owner could make. Straight line means that all your numbers are exactly the same each month and never deviate due to the time of year or the natural flow of the business. Adjust for the seasons and the naturally busy or slow times of the year and show that you understand when money will arrive.

For example, sales for most clubs pick up in late January, followed by a strong period from February to May. Summers are a little slower and then business resumes in the fall after the September holiday and continue strong until Thanksgiving. But if you live in Florida, for example, you might have a strong summer because it is so hot that many people join clubs for the thought of enjoying the air conditioning during the state's hottest months.

Do your research and understand what makes your area unique when it comes to membership sales and the natural flow of the business. Network with other IHRSA members, talk to club owners in cities near where you want to open, and learn when the money arrives in your region of the country.

You fail to use real renewal rates and loss rates.

No one collects all the money from all the members. People quit, get divorced and don't pay, close accounts, and just plain decide not to send you any money. Adjust your plans for losses, and during the second year and beyond, show a normal renewal rate rather than having every member keep going year after year. Use the following basic numbers to get started.

If you are using closed-ended renewals, meaning that you are signing up renewals for one year at a time, show a 40 percent renewal rate. You may do better, but you are looking for a more conservative case. This 40 percent number comes from research and reflects what a typical club will retain in membership in the real world. Losses with auto renewals could be higher. Your target is to retain 60 to 65 percent of all members going into their second year, adjusted for losses. For example:

- A club signs up 100 new memberships in January of 2007.
- The club loses 10 memberships due to the natural collection losses associated with 12-month contracts.
- The club loses 12 memberships due to people moving more than 25 miles from the club, meaning that the club has to cancel the membership per state laws.
- The club would have 78 memberships left at the end of 12 months.

78 x .60 (targeted retention rate) = 47 members

This club started with 100 memberships and started the second year for this group with 47, reflecting a loss rate of 10 percent based upon its membership tool (12-month memberships) and a loss rate of 12 percent based upon people moving outside the club's market. Consider the following numbers as well:

- If you are using 12-month contracts as your base tool, you will lose a little less than 1 percent per month, or 10 percent annually, assuming that you are using a strong third-party financial-service company.
- You will lose at lease 1 percent of your membership per month, or 12 percent annually, to those folks who move more than 25 miles away from the club. The state requires you to cancel those memberships.
- If you are using open-ended memberships, where the member pays as he goes, show 4 to 5 percent per-month loss rates, or 48 to 60 percent annually, although these numbers could be higher in transient or highly competitive markets.
- If you are using auto renewals, meaning that at the end of 12 months your members go from contract to open-ended, use 5 percent monthly losses going into the second year, or 60 percent annually.

IHRSA Tip—How Do I Calculate Membership Retention?

It may seem that "retention" is just an industry buzzword. But before you can brag about your club's sky-high retention rate, you need to know how to calculate it.

Membership retention is measured on an annual basis. Since memberships are added and dropped each month, the retention formula is best calculated using the average opening monthly membership for a rolling 12-month period. The definitions of the attributes are as follows:

Memberships at the beginning of the period (membership accounts)

> **+ New memberships**
> **+ Reinstated memberships that had dropped in previous periods**
> **– Dropped memberships**

Memberships at the end of the period

   Note that this definition excludes all changes between paying membership categories, such as upgrades and downgrades. See Figure 7-1 for a sample calculation.

	Beginning Memberships	Dropped Memberships
January	2,000	60
February	2,025	60
March	2,040	110
April	2,060	75
May	2,090	50
June	2,100	60
July	2,125	60
August	2,130	50
September	2,140	60
October	2,150	70
November	2,175	70
December	2,190	60
Total	25,225	785
Monthly Average = 25,225/12 months = 2,102		
Membership Attrition = 785/2,102 = 37.3%		
Membership Retention = 100% – 37.3% = 62.7%		

Note: This attrition calculation is used and recommended by IHRSA. IHRSA recognizes that health clubs may use other forms of this calculation to track their club needs.

Figure 7-1. Sample membership retention calculation

Membership attrition = (aggregate dropped memberships for 12 months) / (12-month average beginning memberships)
Membership retention = (100% – membership attrition)

A real working budget

Build a budget that reflects a realistic cost of doing business. You should include a sample month of expenses in your business plan, hitting all of the key categories. Figure 7-2, which is used as a monthly management tool as well to control expenses, lists all of the common expenses for a typical club.

Fixed expenses:			
Expense	**Projected**	**Actual**	**+/-**
Rent/mortgage			
Triple net charges			
Yellow pages			
Accounting			
Loan #1			
Loan #2			
Lease #1			
Lease #2			
Other			
Variable expenses:			
Payroll			
Payroll taxes			
Commissions			
Advertising			
Utilities			
Phone			
Printing			
Office supplies			
Cleaning supplies			
Misc. supplies			
Postage			
Nutrition			
Pro shop			
Cooler drinks			
Sports bar/juice bar			
Bars			
Day spa			
Personal/semi-private training			

Figure 7-2. Expense budget management report

Fixed expenses:			
Expense	**Projected**	**Actual**	**+/-**
Variable expenses (cont):			
Tanning			
Childcare			
Group exercise			
Accrual expenses:			
General liability insurance			
Property insurance			
Workman's compensation			
Repair and maintenance			
Education/training			
License/franchise fees			
Capital improvements			
Legal			
Savings/regular			
Savings/accrual			
Totals:	$_____	$_____	$_____

Figure 7-2. Expense budget management report (cont)

The sample projections presented in Figure 7-3 are divided into four sections: general revenue, income from multiple profit centers, operating expenses, and payroll and related expenses. The club is a typical fitness center that might be in the 12,000 to 20,000 square foot range.

Revenue parameters:

- The total membership in the sample presented in Figure 7-3 is projected on a 150-member presale, 150 members during the first month, and 125 members during the second and third months. After that, the club reflects sales that match the demographics and sales history from this owner's first club.

- The 90 percent electronic funds transfer (EFT) refers to 90 percent of the members joining the club and electing to buy some type of membership or payment plan resulting in a contractual obligation for one year. The rule to keep in mind is the 90/10 rule, which states that at least 90 out of every 100 members should elect to join by paying monthly through some type of membership plan, such as EFT, and 10 percent or less should pay in full. If too many pay in full, it reflects a low cash price or heavy discounting by an owner trying to force more members to pay up front. Your business will be healthier if you build a strong receivable base versus trying to get your membership money up front.

- The 6 percent paid-in-full (PIF) is the percentage of members who paid in full for an annual membership (part of the 10 percent in the 90/10 rule).
- The 4 percent is the percentage of members who took short-term memberships as opposed to an annual membership of some type. The short-term membership is paid all at once and is good for up to three months (part of the 10 percent in the 90/10 rule).
- The EFT membership is new sales cash paid as membership fee down payments on the contractual memberships.
- The PIF membership is the total new sales cash for paid-in-full memberships
- Daily fee membership is the amount of daily drop-in cash for the month.
- Short-term membership is the total amount of cash generated in short-term memberships for the month.
- Total new revenue is the total of all income for new sales for the month.
- EFT base is the monthly draft, or billing check, that reflects all of the member payments collected against the contractual obligation.
- Total membership sales are the combination of new sales income produced on a daily basis as sales are made and the total of the monthly check received from the outstanding amount of all the member payments.

Multiple profit center (MPC) parameters:

- Clothing and accessories, supplements, drinks, tanning, personal training, group programming, and juice bar reflect the revenue collected for the month from each of the club's profit centers.
- Total MPC sales are the total of all the revenue from all of the club's profit centers.
- Net income reflects the combination of the revenue from the profit centers and from the revenue section that comes from club membership sales.
- Cost of goods sold is the cost of the profit centers to the club.
- Gross profit is the adjusted net income for the club.

Operating expenses:

- This section reflects the operating expenses for each of these items in the club.
- Total operating expense reflects the total cost of operating, but not the cost of goods sold or payroll and related expenses.

Projections Year 1						
Revenues	Month 1	Month 2	Month 3	Month 4	Month 5	Month 6
Total New Members Projected	150	125	125	115	90	75
Presale: 150 Members						
Total Members	300	398	495	585	674	764
90% EFT	135	113	113	104	81	68
6% PIF	10	8	8	7	6	5
4% Short Term	7	6	6	5	4	3
Daily Fees	15	13	13	12	9	8
EFT Membership $	12,015.00	10,012.50	10,012.50	9,211.50	7,209.00	6,007.50
PIF Membership $	6,903.00	5,752.50	5,752.50	5,292.30	4,141.80	3,451.50
Daily-Fee Membership $	225.00	187.50	187.50	172.50	135.00	112.50
Short-Term Membership $	1,208.25	1,006.88	1,006.88	926.33	724.95	604.13
Total New Revenue	20,351.25	16,959.38	16,959.38	15,602.63	12,210.75	10,175.63
EFT Base	15,930.00	21,107.25	26,284.50	31,047.57	35,810.64	40,573.71
Total Membership Sales	36,281.25	38,066.63	43,243.88	46,650.20	48,021.39	50,749.34
MPC Sales						
Clothing and Accessories	783.29	1,037.86	1,292.43	1,526.63	1,760.83	1,995.03
Supplements	1,174.93	1,556.78	1,938.64	2,289.94	2,641.25	2,992.55
Drinks	308.57	408.85	509.14	601.40	693.66	785.92
Tanning	249.23	330.23	411.23	485.75	560.26	634.78
Personal Training	593.40	786.26	979.11	1,156.54	1,333.96	1,511.39
Group Programming	249.23	330.23	411.23	485.75	560.26	634.78
Juice Bar	1,471.63	1,949.91	2,428.19	2,868.21	3,308.23	3,748.25
Total MPC Sales	4,830.28	6,400.12	7,969.96	9,414.21	10,858.46	12,302.71
Net Income	41,111.53	44,466.74	51,213.83	56,064.40	58,879.85	63,052.05
Cost of Goods Sold	1,869.21	2,476.70	3,084.20	3,643.09	4,201.98	4,760.88
Gross Profit	39,242.32	41,990.04	48,129.63	52,421.31	54,677.87	58,291.17
Operating Expenses						
Advertising	5,600.00	5,600.00	5,600.00	5,600.00	5,600.00	5,600.00
Yellow Pages	700.00	700.00	700.00	700.00	700.00	700.00
Insurance	700.00	700.00	700.00	700.00	700.00	700.00
Outside Services-Janitorial	1,200.00	1,200.00	1,200.00	1,200.00	1,200.00	1,200.00
Accounting/Legal	550.00	550.00	550.00	550.00	550.00	550.00
Printing	525.00	525.00	525.00	525.00	525.00	525.00
Rent	20,979.00	20,979.00	20,979.00	20,979.00	20,979.00	20,979.00
Cleaning Supplies	525.00	525.00	525.00	525.00	525.00	525.00
Repairs/Maintenance	1,400.00	1,400.00	1,400.00	1,400.00	1,400.00	1,400.00
Supplies	350.00	350.00	350.00	350.00	350.00	350.00
Postage	350.00	350.00	350.00	350.00	350.00	350.00
Sales Tax	253.59	336.01	418.42	494.25	570.07	645.89
Telephone	700.00	700.00	700.00	700.00	700.00	700.00
Utilities	2,100.00	2,100.00	2,100.00	2,100.00	2,100.00	2,100.00
Education	1,400.00	1,400.00	1,400.00	1,400.00	1,400.00	1,400.00
Capital Emprovements	2,100.00	2,100.00	2,100.00	2,100.00	2,100.00	2,100.00
Miscellaneous	1,400.00	1,400.00	1,400.00	1,400.00	1,400.00	1,400.00
Total Operating Expenses	40,832.59	40,915.01	40,997.42	41,073.25	41,149.07	41,224.89
Payroll and Related Expenses						
Commission Paid	3,618.75	3,015.63	3,015.63	2,774.38	2,171.25	1,809.38
Salary Expense	23,400.00	23,400.00	23,400.00	23,400.00	23,400.00	23,400.00
Total Payroll and Related Exp.	28,218.75	27,615.63	27,615.63	27,374.38	26,771.25	26,409.38
Total Expenses	68,247.34	64,226.63	64,309.05	64,143.62	63,616.32	63,330.27
Net Income before Taxes	(29,005.02)	(22,236.59)	(16,179.41)	(11,722.31)	(8,938.45)	(5,039.10)

Figure 7-3. Sample projections

Month 7	Month 8	Month 9	Month 10	Month 11	Month 12	Total
75	68	90	75	75	63	
854	944	1033	1123	1213	1283	
68	61	81	68	68	57	
5	4	6	5	5	4	
3	3	4	3	3	3	
8	7	9	8	8	6	
6,007.50	5,406.75	7,209.00	6,007.50	6,007.50	5,046.30	
3,451.50	3,106.35	4,141.80	3,451.50	3,451.50	2,899.26	
112.50	101.25	135.00	112.50	112.50	94.50	
604.13	543.71	724.95	604.13	604.13	507.47	
10,175.63	9,158.06	12,210.75	10,175.63	10,175.63	8,547.53	152,702.21
45,336.78	50,099.85	54,862.92	59,625.99	64,389.06	68,116.68	
55,512.41	59,257.91	67,073.67	69,801.62	74,564.69	76,664.21	665,887.16
2,229.24	2,463.44	2,697.64	2,931.85	3,166.05	3,349.34	
3,343.86	3,695.16	4,046.47	4,397.77	4,749.08	5,024.01	
878.18	970.45	1,062.71	1,154.97	1,247.23	1,319.44	
709.30	783.82	858.34	932.86	1,007.38	1,065.70	
1,688.82	1,866.24	2,043.67	2,221.10	2,398.52	2,537.38	
709.30	783.82	858.34	932.86	1,007.38	1,065.70	
4,188.26	4,628.28	5,068.30	5,508.32	5,948.34	6,292.70	
13,749.97	15,191.22	16,635.47	18,079.72	19,523.98	20,654.26	
69,259.37	74,449.13	83,709.14	87,881.36	94,088.66	97,318.47	821,494.50
5,319.77	5,878.67	6,437.56	6,996.45	7,555.35	7,992.74	
63,939.60	68,570.47	77,271.58	80,884.89	86,533.31	89,325.72	761,227.90
5,600.00	5,600.00	5,600.00	5,600.00	5,600.00	5,600.00	
700.00	700.00	700.00	700.00	700.00	700.00	
700.00	700.00	700.00	700.00	700.00	700.00	
1,200.00	1,200.00	1,200.00	1,200.00	1,200.00	1,200.00	
550.00	550.00	550.00	550.00	550.00	550.00	
525.00	525.00	525.00	525.00	525.00	525.00	
20,979.00	20,979.00	20,979.00	20,979.00	20,979.00	20,979.00	
525.00	525.00	525.00	525.00	525.00	525.00	
1,400.00	1,400.00	1,400.00	1,400.00	1,400.00	1,400.00	
350.00	350.00	350.00	350.00	350.00	350.00	
350.00	350.00	350.00	350.00	350.00	350.00	
721.72	797.54	873.36	949.19	1,025.01	1,084.35	
700.00	700.00	700.00	700.00	700.00	700.00	
2,100.00	2,100.00	2,100.00	2,100.00	2,100.00	2,100.00	
1,400.00	1,400.00	1,400.00	1,400.00	1,400.00	1,400.00	
2,100.00	2,100.00	2,100.00	2,100.00	2,100.00	2,100.00	
1,400.00	1,400.00	1,400.00	1,400.00	1,400.00	1,400.00	
41,300.72	41,376.54	41,452.36	41,528.19	41,604.01	41,663.35	495,117.40
1,809.38	1,628.44	2,171.25	1,809.38	1,809.38	1,519.88	
23,400.00	23,400.00	23,400.00	23,400.00	23,400.00	23,400.00	
26,409.38	26,228.44	26,771.25	26,409.38	26,409.38	26,119.88	26,862.72
63,406.09	63,300.98	63,919.61	63,633.56	63,709.38	63,479.22	322,352.69
53,351.00	5,269.49	13,351.97	17,251.32	22,823.93	25,846.50	(8,044.17)

Projections Year 2 Revenues	Month 1	Month 2	Month 3	Month 4	Month 5	Month 6
Total New Members Projected	104	104	104	115	90	75
Renewals	83	50	50	46	36	30
Total Members	1187	1329	1472	1622	1741	1839
90% EFT	93	93	93	104	81	68
6% PIF	7	7	7	7	6	5
4% Short Term	5	5	5	5	4	3
Daily Fees	10	10	10	12	9	8
EFT Membership $	8,290.35	8,290.35	8,290.35	9,211.50	7,209.00	6,007.50
PIF Membership $	4,763.07	4,763.07	4,763.07	5,292.30	4,141.80	3,451.50
Daily-Fee Membership $	155.25	155.25	155.25	172.50	135.00	112.50
Short-Term Membership $	833.69	833.69	833.69	926.33	724.95	604.13
Total New Revenue	14,042.36	14,042.36	14,042.36	15,602.63	12,210.75	10,175.63
EFT Base	63,007.61	70,574.36	78,141.11	86,152.84	92,422.89	97,647.93
Total Membership Sales	77,049.97	84,616.72	92,183.47	101,755.46	104,633.64	107,823.55
MPC Sales						
Clothing and Accessories	3,098.12	3,470.19	3,842.25	4,236.19	4,544.49	4,801.41
Supplements	4,647.19	5,205.28	5,763.37	6,354.28	6,816.74	7,202.11
Drinks	1,220.47	1,367.04	1,513.61	1,668.80	1,790.25	1,891.46
Tanning	985.77	1,104.15	1,222.53	1,347.88	1,445.97	1,527.72
Personal Training	2,347.06	2,628.93	2,910.79	3,209.23	3,442.80	3,637.43
Group Programming	985.77	1,104.15	1,222.53	1,347.88	1,445.97	1,527.72
Juice Bar	5,820.72	6,519.74	7,218.77	7,958.90	8,538.13	9,020.83
Total MPC Sales	19,105.09	21,399.48	23,693.86	26,123.16	28,024.36	29,608.69
Net Income	96,155.07	106,016.20	115,877.33	127,878.63	132,658.00	137,432.24
Cost of Goods Sold	7,393.25	8281.12	9,169.00	10,109.09	10,844.81	11,457.91
Gross Profit	88,761.82	97,735.07	106,708.33	117,769.54	121,813.19	125,974.33
Operating Expenses						
Advertising	5,600.00	5,600.00	5,600.00	5,600.00	5,600.00	5,600.00
Yellow Pages	700.00	700.00	700.00	700.00	700.00	700.00
Insurance	700.00	700.00	700.00	700.00	700.00	700.00
Outside Services-Janitorial	1,200.00	1,200.00	1,200.00	1,200.00	1,200.00	1,200.00
Accounting/Legal	550.00	550.00	550.00	550.00	550.00	550.00
Printing	525.00	525.00	525.00	525.00	525.00	525.00
Rent	20,979.00	20,979.00	20,979.00	20,979.00	20,979.00	20,979.00
Cleaning Supplies	525.00	525.00	525.00	525.00	525.00	525.00
Repairs/Maintenance	1,400.00	1,400.00	1,400.00	1,400.00	1,400.00	1,400.00
Supplies	350.00	350.00	350.00	350.00	350.00	350.00
Postage	350.00	350.00	350.00	350.00	350.00	350.00
Sales Taxes	1,003.02	1,123.47	1,243.93	1,371.47	1,471.28	1,554.46
Telephone	700.00	700.00	700.00	700.00	700.00	700.00
Utilities	2,100.00	2,100.00	2,100.00	2,100.00	2,100.00	2,100.00
Education	1,400.00	1,400.00	1,400.00	1,400.00	1,400.00	1,400.00
Capital Improvements	2,100.00	2,100.00	2,100.00	2,100.00	2,100.00	2,100.00
Miscellaneous	1,400.00	1,400.00	1,400.00	1,400.00	1,400.00	1,400.00
Total Operating Expenses	41,582.02	41,702.47	41,822.93	41,950.47	42,050.28	42,133.46
Payroll and Related Expenses						
Commission Paid	2,496.94	2,496.94	2,496.94	2,774.38	2,171.25	1,809.38
Salary Expense	23,400.00	23,400.00	23,400.00	23,400.00	23,400.00	23,400.00
Total Payroll and Related Exp.	27,096.94	27,096.94	27,096.94	27,374.38	26,771.25	26,409.38
Total Expenses	67,874.95	64,495.41	64,615.86	65,020.84	64,517.53	64,238.83
Net Income before Taxes	20,886.86	33,239.66	42,092.47	52,748.70	57,295.66	61,735.50

Figure 7-3. Sample projections (cont)

Month 7	Month 8	Month 9	Month 10	Month 11	Month 12	Total
75	68	90	75	75	63	
30	27	36	30	30	25	
1937	2026	2144	2242	2341	2423	
68	61	81	68	68	57	
5	4	6	5	5	4	
3	3	4	3	3	3	
8	7	9	8	8	6	
6,007.50	5,406.75	7,209.00	6,007.50	6,007.50	5,046.30	
3,451.50	3,106.35	4,141.80	3,451.50	3,451.50	2,899.26	
112.50	101.25	135.00	112.50	112.50	94.50	
604.13	543.71	724.95	604.13	604.13	507.47	
10,175.63	9,158.06	12,210.75	10,175.63	10,175.63	8,547.53	140,599.30
102,872.97	107,575.50	113,845.55	119,070.59	124,295.63	128,684.66	
113,048.59	116,733.56	126,056.30	129,246.22	134,471.26	137,232.19	1,324,850.94
5,058.33	5,289.55	5,597.86	5,854.77	6,111.69	6,327.50	
7,587.49	7,934.33	8,396.78	8,782.16	9,167.54	9,491.26	
1,992.67	2,083.76	2,205.22	2,306.43	2,407.64	2,492.65	
1,609.47	1,683.04	1,781.14	1,862.88	1,944.63	2,013.30	
3,832.07	4,007.24	4,240.80	4,435.44	4,630.07	4,793.56	
1,609.47	1,683.04	1,781.14	1,862.88	1,944.63	2,013.30	
9,503.52	9,937.95	10,517.18	10,999.88	11,482.58	11,888.04	
31,193.02	32,618.92	34,520.11	36,104.45	37,688.78	39,019.61	359,099.53
144,241.61	149,352.48	160,576.41	165,350.66	172,160.03	176,251.80	1,683,950.46
12,071.01	12,622.80	13,358.52	13,971.62	14,584.72	15,099.73	
132,170.60	136,729.68	147,217.89	151,379.04	157,575.31	161,152.07	1,544,986.89
5,600.00	5,600.00	5,600.00	5,600.00	5,600.00	5,600.00	
700.00	700.00	700.00	700.00	700.00	700.00	
700.00	700.00	700.00	700.00	700.00	700.00	
1,200.00	1,200.00	1,200.00	1,200.00	1,200.00	1,200.00	
550.00	550.00	550.00	550.00	550.00	550.00	
525.00	525.00	525.00	525.00	525.00	525.00	
20,979.00	20,979.00	20,979.00	20,979.00	20,979.00	20,979.00	
525.00	525.00	525.00	525.00	525.00	525.00	
1,400.00	1,400.00	1,400.00	1,400.00	1,400.00	1,400.00	
350.00	350.00	350.00	350.00	350.00	350.00	
350.00	350.00	350.00	350.00	350.00	350.00	
1,637.63	1,712.49	1,812.31	185.48	1,978.66	2,048.53	
700.00	700.00	700.00	700.00	700.00	700.00	
2,100.00	2,100.00	2,100.00	2,100.00	2,100.00	2,100.00	
1,400.00	1,400.00	1,400.00	1,400.00	1,400.00	1,400.00	
2,100.00	2,100.00	2,100.00	2,100.00	2,100.00	2,100.00	
1,400.00	1,400.00	1,400.00	1,400.00	1,400.00	1,400.00	
42,216.63	42,291.49	42,391.31	40,764.48	42,557.66	42,627.53	504,090.73
1,809.38	1,628.44	2,171.25	1,809.38	1,809.38	1,519.88	
23,400.00	23,400.00	23,400.00	23,400.00	23,400.00	23,400.00	
26,409.38	26,228.44	26,771.25	26,409.38	26,409.38	26,119.88	320,193.54
64,322.01	64,215.93	64,858.56	64,579.86	64,663.04	64,443.40	777,846.22
67,848.59	72,513.75	82,359.34	86,799.18	92,912.27	96,708.67	767,140.66

Payroll and related expenses:

- Commission paid is for sales and other bonuses paid to the employees
- Salary expense is for all employees and includes the owner's compensation if he is taking a normal manager's salary.
- Total payroll and related expense is the total payroll and supporting expenses for the club.
- Total expense is the combined operating and payroll expense for the club.
- Net income is pretax net for the month (EBIT)

Bank and investor considerations

This section of the prospectus shows what's in it for the investor and demonstrates your ability to pay back the bank. It is based upon the preceding section of projections that should build in the anticipated bank payment or payments to the investors.

Most investors stay away from a business deal that gives them equity only in a gym business. The numbers are too small and they have too many other options with less risk.

A common method of attracting an investor is to offer a combination of equity and return on investment (ROI). For example, an investor might put up $250,000 for 25 percent of a gym that will have a million-dollar start-up cost. This investor would be paid back $125,000 over seven years as ROI, at an aggressive interest rate, and the other $125,000 would stay in the business as part of the investor's equity. This possibility is just a starting point for your negotiations, and your deal with your investors may end up being different, but just remember that your investor wants both equity and return from the deal.

Payment to investors should be included in the projection to demonstrate the ability to repay. Anticipated investor notes should also be discussed to demonstrate that they are built into the club's operating budget and are part of cash-flow needs.

Who will own and operate the business?

This section gives an investor an idea of who is going to run the club and if the team has any experience or the expertise to run this project. If the owner has been successful before, then this is an easy section to complete and is based on a simple resume of the owner's experience and qualifications. If you have not been in the fitness business before, real-life business qualifications are the most important thing, followed by any education or work experience you might have to prepare for owning an expensive fitness business financed by someone else's money.

Summary of the project

The summary section should tie the entire package together. Many loan officers will read the summary first and then start at the beginning to see if the data matches the claims at the end.

To be successful in obtaining a loan, you must be prepared and organized when making your request. You must know exactly how much money you need, why you need it, and how you will pay it back. On top of all of this material, you must convince your lender that you are a good credit risk.

The summary should be used to convey information that gives the lender confidence in the fact that you know your numbers and have researched the project. If they like what they read in the short form, they might want you to gather additional information.

A Sample Prospectus

The sample that follows was designed for an actual club with an existing owner who was seeking SBA or conventional financing. This prospectus is the tool she used to gather investors and to make her presentation at the bank.

Cover page

Prospectus for a new fitness facility

Proposed business
The American Workout Company
Highway 9 and Route 3
Your town, your state

Owned by a newly formed partnership
Operated by Sarah Smith
Owner of the existing American Workout Company

Submitted for review November, 2007

Sarah Smith
230 North Addison
Your town, your state 12345
321-555-1234

Overview of the project/executive summary

This project will be a 14,000-square-foot adult-alternative gym located on Highway 9 and Route 3 in (your town, your state). In this case, adult-alternative is defined as a gym built to appeal to the top 60 percent of the area's demographic package. This upscale approach will be reflected in the degree of finish and the programming offered in the club as compared to other facilities currently in the area.

The gym will be owned and operated by Sarah Smith, a successful gym owner who currently operates the American Workout Company, located at 2214 South Main in (your town). Financing for the project will be through the combination of a partnership and either conventional or SBA financing.

The proposed site is currently raw land and comprises 2.7 acres. The property is listed at $900,000, has a 250-foot frontage to Route 3, and would require minimum site preparation.

The projected total cost of the project will be $3,151,000. A partnership group is being formed that will put up the initial cash needed for financing.

This area, referred to as the Highlands, has 67,000 residents meeting our demographic requirements within a five-mile ring from the site. At the current location, 87 percent of the members come from within the five-mile ring of the club. If marketed properly, a club has the ability to attract approximately 3.5 to 4 percent of the population within the five-mile ring. The demographics in the area give more than enough qualified prospective members to operate a successful health club.

Assuming that financing for the project will be done by the first of the year, the new gym will open in December, 2007, which allows for proper time for staff training and marketing before the New Year. The project was estimated at only nine months, but December allows for at least a two-month overrun.

The club and property will be separate partnerships. Sarah Smith was seeking long-term equity partners in the property who will control an 80 percent stake. In the gym, the partners will represent a 40 percent position. The partners will be asked for 20 percent of the total cost of the project as their buy-in, depending on the final type of financing decided upon.

Sarah Smith has already done the groundwork for a 504 SBA loan, although the bankers that have been interviewed up to this point are sugesting conventional financing for 20 years. The total cost for the project will be $3,151,000.

Club model

An upscale adult club will cater to people in the 25- to 45-year-old range that have a household income of at least $50,000. This style of club is breaking away from the traditional model offered in this area, reflected by out-of-date equipment, cheap prices, weak programming, poor design, and cheap finish. The area and its residents have no choice when it comes to seeking an upscale facility.

This club will have a very upscale finish, a juice bar that will cater to members as well as a street population, and a sports-activity and conditioning department catering to lifestyle enhancement such as golf improvement and weight management. The club will also offer the Body Training System®, a state-of-the-art group exercise system from New Zealand.

The goal for the first 12 months of operation is to achieve an active membership base of a little over 900 members, which is a number adjusted for losses and club cancellations. The club will be built upon a strong receivable base foundation and profit centers that allow the club to make money from the members it already has in the system. The club pricing will be $90 as a one-time membership fee and monthly dues of $49 per month. The club will also use The Club Financial Services from (any town, any state), as its third-party collection and service system. The Club is the category leader in the industry for this service and services 9 percent of all the clubs in the country.

Currently in the industry, a health club's revenue mix is 95 percent membership workout-based and five percent multiple-profit-center-based. This data means that most clubs are too dependent on generating new memberships every day and has no cash flow from its existing membership base.

This club will be designed to take full advantage of the members it has coming through its doors each day. The goal for the club is $5 per day in income from the members who are working out. This number is not related to any monies they might have paid to work out, such as a monthly fee or drop-in payment.

The club will have a Juice Company license for its juice bar as the central social focus in the club. This set-up will allow for sales to the members as well as developing a traffic flow from the street. The club will also have an Ultra Weight Loss Management program that allows for revenue from nutrition guidance and training support. Other profit centers will be drink coolers, tanning, and basic clothing, all of which have been proven in a health club environment.

The foundation of the club's image will be its trial membership marketing. The club will allow potential members to try the club before they purchase a membership. This type of marketing puts the emphasis on the club's operations, not on salesmanship alone, allowing the club to get a higher monthly fee from its members as compared to other clubs in town.

Estimated costs of the proposed gym

The following costs are based on acquiring the land and building a 14,000-square-foot building on the property. The actual building will have a footprint of 11,000 square feet and a mezzanine of 3,000 square feet.

Land costs. The land can be acquired for a cost of $900,000 and is 2.7 acres. The lot has a frontage of 250 feet on Highway 3 and has high visibility on the front of the property and slopes toward the rear of the site. The building can be placed on the front of the site for maximum visibility for the business and parking can be situated in the rear. Highway 3 has a daily traffic count of 27,000 cars, which is considered high for this area.

Building costs. Joseph Angelo, a noted architect from New Jersey specializing in fitness businesses, has been contracted to design the building. He will work with Manny Jackson, a local architect who will do the site plan in conjunction with Angelo. The estimated cost for a steel building with a custom front is $60 per square foot, based on an 11,000-square-foot footprint. This cost will include the shell, HVAC, proper electrical, and plumbing for this type of business and the mezzanine structure. This cost does not include internal finish or equipment. Total building cost is $660,000.

Site preparation. Initial site preparation for the site was projected at $200,000. This cost will give the property 140 parking places and allow for the development of a retention pond at the rear of the property.

Build-out costs. This club will be an upscale adult club designed for the top 60 percent of the demographic market. For that reason, this club will require a slightly higher degree of finish than a typical club in this area. The initial estimate for build-out for this project is $50 per square foot, or $550,000 for the project.

Equipment costs. The equipment costs for this facility will be projected at $332,000. This cost includes all strength and cardio equipment for the facility, but not entertainment theater, group exercise, or specialty costs.

Special note. To determine equipment costs, use the following formula:

- For the first 10,000 square feet, use $30,000 per thousand.
- For every thousand after the initial 10,000, use $8,000 per thousand.
- In this example, the club would have an initial cost of $300,000 for the first 10,000 square feet and $32,000 for the other 4,000 square feet.

Reserve capital. The club is scheduled to open in December 2007, which is the prime month to open a club. According to that opening date, the club will begin to cover its own expenses approximately nine months from the first of the year, or in September. Based on that timeframe, the club will need two months base operating expense (BOE) in reserve. BOE for this club will run $75,000 per month, meaning that the club will need $150,000 in reserve capital.

General category. The club will need initial inventory, desks, computers, and other general items to open that are not part of build-out or equipment. Based on a 14,000-square-foot club, the initial budget for these items will be $81,000.

Special note. To figure general category items, use the following formula:

- For the first 10,000 square feet, use $7500 per thousand.
- For every thousand after the initial 10,000, use $1,500 per thousand.
- In this example, the club would have an initial cost of $75,000 for the first 10,000 square feet and $6,000 for the other 4,000 square feet.

Marketing costs. The club will do a 30-day soft sale in December and an aggressive campaign during the first 90 days the club is open. During the presale, the club will spend approximately $8,000 in direct mail marketing, and the club will budget another $30,000 in marketing dollars for the first 90 days. Total marketing costs will be $38,000.

Architectural fees. Architectural fees include design and interior as well as onsite visits by Angelo. Fees are estimated at $240,000.

Total project costs.

- Land costs: $900,000
- Building costs: $660,000
- Site preparation: $200,000
- Build-out: $550,000
- Equipment costs: $332,000
- Reserve capital: $150,000
- General category items: $81,000
- Marketing for presale and first 90 days: $38,000
- Architectural fees: $240,000

Total project cost: $3,151,000

Proposed financing

Two types of financing are being considered for this project: conventional financing with 20 percent down over 20 years and an SBA 504 with 10 percent down and a 20-year payback. The result of initial discussions with several bankers concerning the project points the project toward conventional financing.

Partners are involved in both scenarios. A partnership is being formed to acquire both the building and the property, which will result in two separate ownership groups. The partners will put up the initial percentage for either type of loan, which will be repaid through the profits of the business.

The building partnership will consist of the following people:

- Sarah Smith: 20 percent
- Jim Johnson, a local contractor: 30 percent
- Randall Washington, a pro athlete who works out at the current club: 30 percent
- Johnny Sindell, an independent investor and current member: 10 percent
- Susan Vaughn, an independent investor and current member: 10 percent

The gym partnership will consist of the following people:

- Sarah Smith: 60 percent
- Jim Johnson, Randall Washington, Johnny Sindell, and Susan Vaughn: 10 percent each

The partnership was formed to take part in this project as a long-term real estate investment. Sarah Smith will acquire 20 percent of the building and property as operating partner. The partnership will allow Sarah Smith a larger percentage of the gym business for her role as onsite operating manager.

The partnership is seeking a loan of $2,500,000 at 9 percent over 25 years. This loan would result in a payment of $20,979, well within the operating parameters of the budget. The total project is planned for $3,151,000 with a down payment of approximately 21 percent, or $651,000. The down payment will be cash raised by the partners.

A one-month BOE for the American Workout Company

- Rent/mortgage payment: $20,979
- Payroll: $28,000
- Advertising: $5600

- Utilities: $2100
- Phone: $700
- Yellow Pages ad: $700
- Accounting: $300
- Printing: $525
- Office supplies: $350
- Cleaning supplies: $525
- Postage: $350
- All insurances: $700
- Apex Fitness: $2500
- Basic clothing: $1500
- Drinks: $1500
- Juice bar: $1500
- Tanning: $600
- Repair and maintenance: $1400
- Education and training: $1400
- Capital improvement: $2100
- Legal: $250
- Miscellaneous: $1400

Total monthly base operating expense: $74,979

Bank and investor considerations

The total cost of the project is estimated at $3,151,000. The partnership will put up 21 percent, or $651,000 in cash. The projected loan amount will be $2,500,000 at 9 percent over 25 years.

Based on these numbers, the club will only have a $20,979 payment per month. If the club were renting in the same area, it would be paying $12 per foot plus triple net. At this cost, the projected rent for the same site would be $14,000 per month plus an estimated triple net number of about $2.50 a foot, or another $2900 per month, for a total of $16,900.

For a difference of only about $4000 per month, the partners will have a long-term investment, tax benefits, and the ability to refinance in the future to keep the facility current. This long-term investment was what attracted the investors to the project in the first place.

The partners are looking for a long-term investment and will not take anything out of the building partnership. They are in fact looking for the business to carry the note on the property and will not participate in the business except as needed financially in the future.

Only bonuses based on the profitability of the club will be offered to investors in the club partnership. No other participation or salaries will be offered. Sarah Smith will be paid a managing partner's salary capped at $75,000 per year and will participate in bonuses paid on profits.

The partnership has agreed to invest in another club once this club has shown itself to be at least 20 percent net profitable before taxes on a monthly basis for six consecutive months. The partnership has initially agreed to fund up to five additional clubs if the units meet the minimum profitability needed.

Operating team for the club

Sarah Smith has been a successful club operator for three years. She is a graduate of the University of Arkansas in business and has completed several graduate-level courses.

She has completed two Thomas Plummer and Company (TPC) weeklong training seminars on advanced club operations and has attended three TPC two-day management seminars. She has also attended two IHRSA national conferences and is a current member with the organization.

Her current club has been profitable since its inception has been expanded once since it was opened using cash from operations. The club currently has a receivable base held by The Club Financial Services valued at $425,000. Current loans are held by First Federal of (your town) and are current.

Thomas Jenkins will be the manager of the club. He has been assistant manager in the current club for two years and has been training to take over the new facility.

Thomas is a graduate of the University of Michigan in sports management. He has graduated from a Thomas Plummer Company weeklong advanced school and has also completed an advanced sales training seminar by the same company.

Jim Johnson is a local contractor who has been in the community for more than 15 years.

Randall Washington is a pro athlete who has played professional basketball for the last six years and is from the local community.

Johnny Sindell is a local investor and member of the current club. He is the owner of several restaurants in the area.

Sarah Vaughn is a local investor and member of the current club.

Summary of the project

This proposal is for a new upscale health club in (your town) that will open in late 2007. The club fills a need for a quality club and has no competitors in the upper end of the marketplace. The club will specialize in members in the 25- to 45-year-old range.

According to American Sports Data, the mores important demographic trend is the growth of members aged 35 to 54, which skyrocketed 55 percent from 1987 to 1998, while the 18- to 34-year-old group only produced a 20 percent growth in the same period.

All competitors in the (your town) area are concentrating on the younger markets and no one yet has built a club seeking an older and more affluent population. This club will have the finish, programming, and profit centers that cater to a wealthier and older membership.

The demographics in the area support the membership needed for a club of this type. Approximately 67,000 households are located within five miles of the club that have an average household income of over $50,000.

The project has been estimated at $3,151,000 by one of the premier architects in the club industry, who has build more than 350 clubs in his career. The club will seek conventional financing and has built a partnership to contribute 20 percent down. The partners are all successful businesspeople in their own right and are looking for a real estate investment that is passive based on the club business paying the note payment.

A successful businesswoman who has run a profitable fitness business similar to the new project for more than three years will operate the club. During that time, she has trained a staff and management team to run both projects.

The partnership would like to have all loan packages completed and funding in place by the first of the year, allowing for a full 12 months to build and open the gym. This timeline allows for at least a two-month overrun for the build-out and completion of the project. Demographic data, club plans, and additional financial information are available upon request.

Tips for People Seeking Loans and Investors

- Interview more than one banker if it is your first project. Tell them you would like to submit a loan proposal and ask about various loans and what they like to see in a project.
- You will have to show some type of personal participation. Very seldom can you do an entire project without having some personal money involved. Even

investors like to see at least $50,000 on the table. The investors might put up the rest, but they also like to know that you are vested in the project.

- Leave the ball cap at the door. You are there to borrow money, and ties or dresses are considered proper business clothes. You are dealing with very conservative people who like to loan money to other conservative people.

- Contact IHRSA. You should be a member of IHRSA, as is mentioned in the resource guide at the end of the book. This group has many publications that can add to your loan package, such as the *IHRSA Guide to the Health Club Industry for Lenders and Investors* (2nd ed.).

- Get a job in the business first. If you are new to the industry, go get a job in a gym and learn how to sell a membership. If you are not willing to take this step, then don't get in the gym business. Even if you have a lot of money and have been successful somewhere else, learn to sell somebody something in this business before you invest.

- Be prepared. As mentioned earlier, very few owners can defend their business plans. Understand how cash flow works and be able to discuss every aspect of the business. Again, if you have never worked in a gym, this discussion will be short, followed by a "no" from the lender.

- Almost everyone started with their family first. It's the rare owner that didn't have some type of family help to get that first gym opened. Consider a family partnership for the first club.

- Investors are more interested in the real estate than they are in owning a gym. Owning your own building often makes more sense to investors, and is better for your long-term future, in most cases, than renting and putting all that money in some else's space. It is easier to attract investors if they are gaining a passive investment such as a building with a built-in tenant. It is like buying a great rental house and having a tenant that paints the place and even does his own plumbing. He pays rent while you get appreciation. Investors look at the gym business in the same way. They own the real estate, you make the payments, and it becomes a passive appreciation-growing business deal.

- Give up a lot to get your first gym, but make sure you can't get kicked out of your own business. If you have nothing and investors want a large portion of your business to do it, then go for it. Give up 60 percent if you get 40 percent with little of your own money, but make sure your attorney structures the partnership deal so you can't get kicked out of your own business.

- A loan may be as simple as having a cosigner. You may need less cash but a stronger cosigner to get into your first gym. Ask your lender about what it would take to involve a cosigner.

- Look for used gyms. Have a lawyer send a blind letter, meaning that his name is on it, but not yours, to every gym in your target area. The letter states that the lawyer represents a qualified buyer wishing to purchase a gym in the area. You may get no responses or a few outlandish dream deals, but you might also get the real thing. Most used gyms are absurdly overpriced, but start there and see what's in the market. The valuation section in Chapter 3 may help you get a better idea of what a gym is worth.

- Build smaller than you think. Some excellent gyms are 1300 square feet and make the owners a decent salary and got them into the business. Most first gyms are too much for the market, since the owners had too long to think about building the perfect gym. Start smaller, as you can always expand or build a second unit later. One of the dumbest things heard from even experienced owners is, "I have to build a gym that big. If it's too small it will get too crowded." In other words, you are too successful and the gym is too popular—a tough problem easily remedied by another unit or expansion. Remember that the gym of the future, because of the increasing start-up costs, will be a smaller more-intimate delivery system probably in the 5,000 to 20,000 square-foot range.

The Key Concept in This Chapter

If you want money, you're going have to build a business plan. The model included in this chapter can be your reference point when you first get started. If you want more help beyond what is included in this chapter, turn to the reference section at the end of the book.

Additional Resource

McCarthy, J. (2004). *The IHRSA Guide to Bank Financing.* Boston, MA: IHRSA.
www.ihrsastore.com

IHRSA Tip—Cap Ex: How Much Is Enough?

What is cap ex? Cap ex (capital expense) is a broader expense category than "depreciation." Depreciation, technically, is a noncash expense relating to the continually decreasing value of fixed assets by reason of time, wear and tear, and the continually changing nature of every marketplace.

Cap ex is a real expense, a cash expense. It includes depreciation, but it also includes improvements, such as a new yoga studio, additional fitness equipment, a new front desk design, a new software package, an expansion of the parking lot, etc.

What percent of revenue should be allocated to cap ex? A cap ex budget that will keep a club vigorously competitive over a 10-year period does not follow a straight-line formula. One way to budget cap ex is by determining the percentage of revenue that needs to be allocated to this expense on an annual basis. Using the "percentage of revenue" method, and allowing for all the factors relating to wear and tear and essential improvements, a sensible cap ex budget might look as follows:

- Year 1: 0 percent
- Year 2: 3 percent
- Year 3: 4 percent
- Year 4: 10 to 15 percent
- Year 5: 4 percent
- Year 6: 4 percent
- Year 7: 4 percent
- Year 8: 20 to 25 percent
- Year 9: 4 percent
- Year 10: 4 percent

Using this formula, if you take the mean expense for years 4 and 8, the average annual cap ex over a 10-year period would be approximately 6 to 6.5 percent.

Why the spikes in years 4 and 8? Every three to five years, the market takes a significant turn or, put another way, it makes a significant advance. Whenever such advances occur, a cap ex adjustment is required. For example, about five years ago, it became clear that yoga and Pilates were going to become mainstays of the club business. And five years before that, Spinning became a major industry trend. No club can afford to miss these opportunities. Yet, doing them properly requires an investment "spike." If you do not budget these spikes, then change becomes a threat rather than an opportunity.

Then, at least every eight to 10 years, a health club, as is the case with any other retail business, needs a total overhaul so that it can once again become a "brand new" facility. Otherwise, the club will become old, dated, and marginal, and can be severely harmed by any new competitor.

What other methods can be used to calculate cap ex? The "cost per square foot" method has been successfully employed by many clubs. Using this method, and excluding large court areas (tennis, racquetball, squash) from the calculation, a reasonable annual cap ex for most clubs might approximate $2.00 to $2.50 per square foot. Thus, for a 30,000-square-foot club, this method would require an allocation of $60,000 to $75,000 (annual average over a 10-year period).

Do these formulas always work? A key factor in determining cap ex is revenue per square foot. These formulas will work for most clubs that fall in the normal range with respect to revenue per square foot (i.e., $40 to $60 annual revenue/total indoor square feet). However, for clubs that generate significantly greater revenue, adjustments need to be made. The adjustments would be to a lower percentage for clubs using the "percent of revenue" method, and to a higher dollar amount for those using the "cost per square foot" method.

For example, for a club generating $100 per square foot in revenue, the annual cap ex budget might be 4 percent rather than 6 percent of revenues, and, at the same time, it might be $3.75 per square foot rather than $2.50. In any situation, however, market conditions can change rapidly. Whenever this situation occurs, a cap ex plan, no matter how well-conceived, may need to be reevaluated.

What if you budget less? Some very bright people in the industry would argue that annual cap ex can and should be lower. And others who are equally bright who would place it higher. However, the risk of underbudgeting cap ex is greater than the risk of overbudgeting it. The risks of underbudgeting cap ex can be severe. Club members and frontline club personnel are keenly aware when clubs begin to deteriorate. Whenever this happens, a club can rapidly become less competitive with respect to neighboring facilities. You want both your members and your staff to be proud of your facility. And your members notice when they see you continually investing in improvements.

What else should you know? Probably the most important thing about cap ex is not simply what you do, but how well you get the word out. Whenever a club makes improvements, it should have a comprehensive strategy to trumpet those improvements to the local media, current members, prospective members, and the community as a whole. How you leverage cap ex is as important as the money you spend on it.

One final word: Please use these formulas as guidelines, not as rules. Your own sense of what must to be done (on an annual basis, as well as periodically) to make your club as dynamic as possible needs to be your primary guiding principle. The general guidelines specified in this tip are meant to serve as background data for your own, more experiential judgments.

8

Building a Strong Receivable Base

Club owners should be seeking long-term stability, the ability to project revenues into the future, the capacity to have cash flow during slight downturns in the business, and most importantly, the ability to increase the worth of the business and sell it in the future at a gain if or when they decide to get out of the business. Only one method can accomplish all of these financial goals, and that is the development of a strong receivable base based on consistent member payments.

You must first understand just what a receivable base really is. A receivable base can be understood in several ways, but the simplest way is by thinking of it as how much money you could count on collecting in the future from your current members if you never sold another membership in your club.

The key phrases are "count on" and "future." For a receivable base to exist, an obligation must be present between the member and the club. If no obligation exists, then the club owner has nothing to count on at a later date.

For example, an older-style club that sells the majority of its memberships as paid-in-full does not have a receivable base because no revenue can be projected into the future. The owner received cash today, spent the cash today, and must sell memberships in the future to have revenue in the future.

This same scenario applies to club owners who build their membership based on open ended, month-to-month memberships. These owners do have cash flow in the form of a monthly check from the total of their member payments, but they don't have a true receivable base because they can't count on revenue in the future. The nature of being month-to-month means that if the entire membership decided to leave tomorrow it could do so by simply calling their banks and canceling the monthly draft, if the club was using some form of electronic funds transfer (EFT) (Figure 8-1).

Clubs offer Consumers a Choice of Membership Plans		
	% of clubs offering	% of accounts per plan (mean)
Month-to-month	76%	49%
12 months, convert to monthly upon month 13	47%	29%
12 months, renew for 12 months	48%	18%
Longer than 12 months	21%	5%

Data from a sample of IHRSA North American Health Clubs, 2006. Profiles of Success, 2006

Figure 8-1. Examples of the types of membership plans offered by clubs and used by consumers

This type of club seldom loses its entire membership in one swift shot, but it can often lose 30 to 40 percent of its membership in a 90-day period if a fresh, bright competitor moves across the street. Without obligation, meaning that the member has some type of commitment to pay the club in the future, such as a 12-month contract, the club doesn't have the stability that a similar club would have with a strong receivable base.

Another way to look at a receivable base is that the club sells memberships over time, meaning that it adds new members each month that it is open, and the accumulation of the monthly payments each member makes over the length of his contract or commitment to belong to the gym grows to a certain point, providing stability for the club owner in the form of a monthly cash. This stable cash flow becomes the club's most valuable asset, because it is something that bankers will recognize and loan against as compared to equipment or the number of members a club claims to have, both of which have little meaning to a bank because they are worthless if the club owner should fail.

Consider the following example. A 13,000-square-foot club opens with a $59 per-month membership and a 12-month obligation (annual contract), for a total annual membership of $708. This example ignores any type of one-time membership fee because you are only concerned with the receivable base, not the money a club would get up front for its memberships.

If the club enrolled 90 members a month for 12 months it would have a gross membership of 1080 at the end of the year. But, in real life, owners never collect all of the money from all of the members. Loss rates are inevitable and need to be subtracted.

Loss rates are discussed in detail later in this chapter, but you can look at the 1080 members and determine how this number would be affected. First of all, not everyone pays as promised, creating one type of loss rate that will affect the total. By using 12-month contracts, which have the highest chance of being collected, this club would only lose about 10 percent of its membership due to nonpayment.

The club would also lose another 12 percent due to cancellations. This type of cancellation would be due to either a member moving too far from the club, or because of a medical, death, or three-day right of cancellation, which is a cooling off period the members can use to escape any type of retail installment contract, such as a 12-month membership on a contractual basis at a club. The total of these two numbers is 22 percent, which means that a 22 percent adjustment must be made to the members paying the club.

1080 gross members x 0.78 collection rate =
842 members paying at year's end

When these members make their $59 monthly payment, the club would receive a gross check before collection expenses of $49,678. This gross check would be adjusted by about 7 percent, which is the national average for clubs using a sophisticated third-party financial system, such as those listed in the IHRSA directory. These companies specialize in servicing membership contracts for people who own and operate fitness businesses. These companies can, for example, collect the member payments for you, install member-tracking software, chase members who don't pay as promised, and provide data and reporting that help a club owner make more informed decisions.

The power in these companies is that they usually collect more from the same member base than you can do yourself, which is true for many reasons. These companies have the illusion of power and many members feel obligated to pay when they make their other major payments, such as a car payment or mortgage.

These companies also specialize in the fitness business and have the systems in place, and know the collection laws, to be able to collect the most money from the members you have in the state where you live and operate. An economy of scale also exists with these companies that a small operator with less than 25 clubs would find hard to duplicate. Therefore, this owner would spend more to collect from the members than it would cost to pay a professional to do so.

A degree of vulnerability comes with collecting your own memberships. If an employee dies or a small team quits, your business is at risk because you are dependent on too few people handling your most important asset, which is your club's receivable base.

Therefore, you should always use a third-party financial-service company to handle your memberships. If you do so, the net amount to the club after the national average of 7 percent, which includes EFT members (less expensive to the club), as well as those members who decide to write checks each month to pay for their membership (more expensive to the club, but you still need to offer the option), would be calculated as follows:

$49,678 x 0.93 (7% collection fee) = $46,200

Projected as part of a *total outstanding receivable base*, which represents the total amount of member payments the club owner can count on being collected in the future, because an obligation is in place in the form of a 12-month contract between the member and the club, the total to be collected from all member payments would be approximately $550,000 to $600,000 after collection expenses. This number is defined as the club's total outstanding receivables, or receivable base.

Going further, this club also has a monthly base operating expense (BOE) of $60,000, which includes all bills the club pays each month, including payroll, taxes, cost of goods, debt service, and any other bills the club has to cover to reach its monthly break-even point. The exception would be if the owner is offsite and has a manager. In this example, the owner's salary would not be counted as part of the club's BOE.

The Single Most Important Number to Look at in Your Business

A relationship exists between the monthly BOE and the net amount of the monthly member payments, or receivable check. Once the net check gets to a point that a certain percentage of expense is automatically met each month, the club has reached a level of stability and maturity that will allow it to withstand heavy competition as well as any serious downturns in member sales.

Your goal is 70 percent coverage of your monthly BOE by your net receivable check.

Using this example, the club's BOE is $60,000 per month. A 70 percent coverage goal would mean that the club's goal for its net receivable check would be $42,000 per month. The club in this example has a net check of $46,000, which represents a very stable and financially secure business. For example:

$46,000 net check/$60,000 BOE = 76 percent

A relationship exists between the monthly BOE and the net amount of the monthly member payments, or receivable check.

This percentage of coverage could happen as early as month 13 for a new club and should happen no later than month 25. Existing clubs that are revamping their existing receivable base and pricing structure as discussed in this book should make reaching 70 percent coverage of their BOE by their net monthly receivable check one of the prime goals for their business.

The ultimate goal, of course, is to grow your net receivable check to the point that it covers 100 percent of your monthly expenses. In such a comfortable business world, you receive your check on the first of the month and your club is immediately profitable for the month. Every dollar you make from that point forward is profit. From research conducted by the Thomas Plummer Company, only about 5 to 6 percent of the clubs in the country reach this goal. It is, however, *the* goal to strive for in your club business.

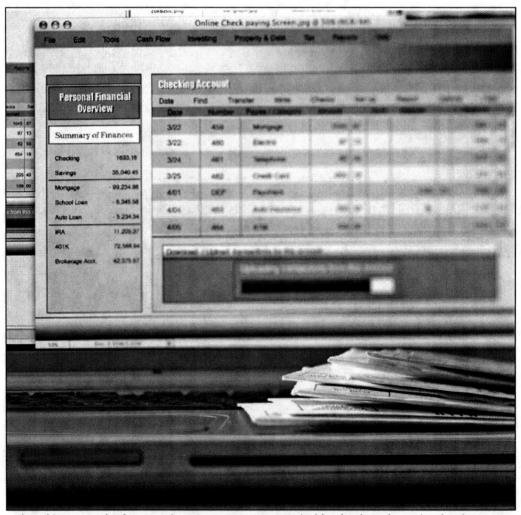

The ultimate goal, of course, is to grow your net receivable check to the point that it covers 100 percent of your monthly expenses.

The Difference Between Obligation and Method of Payment

A common point of confusion for many owners is the difference between setting an obligation for the member and the member's method of payment. The actual point of confusion arises when owners start to use EFT for collecting their member payments.

Method of payment refers to how the member actually makes his payment each month for his membership. A member may give a club actual cash, write a check, or allow the club to automatically draft (withdraw funds electronically from a checking, savings, or credit card) each month.

EFT as a method of payment means that the member will, for the sake of convenience, allow the club owner to automatically take the payment each month electronically from his account or credit card. *This arrangement does not infer obligation.*

Having 1000 members on EFT each month does ensure good cash flow. It does not, however, mean that the club has any implied obligation between the member and the club unless the club has established a 12-month contract first and then let the member pay by their desired method of payment. In other words, without first establishing a contract between the member and club that promises payment for a fixed period of time, such as 12 months, the club owner has not developed a strong receivable base by enrolling the member on EFT payments. The member can still walk away by simply calling his bank if he has not first signed a contract for obligation.

The rule of thumb is to first establish an obligation (contract) and then let the new member pick his own method of payment. The contract builds a receivable base, the main goal of selling club memberships, and the member makes his payments using a method he feels meets his individual needs. The right flow, or order, for a club membership is as follows:

- The club establishes a pricing system that is fair to the member, yet allows the club to collect the most money from the most members while developing a strong receivable base.

- This pricing system is first built upon the 12-month contract, which is fair to the member yet collectable for the club. These 12-month contracts only have approximately a 10 percent national loss rate annually if collected by a strong third-party financial service company. This method establishes obligation first.

- Once the new member agrees to the obligation, the club then offers method of payment. For example, the club's monthly price might be $49 per month if the club may automatically deduct the payment from the member's checking account or credit card. If the member wishes to write a check each month instead, something at least half your members will choose if given a choice, the club might charge $54 per month, passing along the slightly higher charge of servicing a check with the third-party financial-service company as opposed to EFT.

- The club should have established a relationship with a third-party financial-service company (data management company) to be the hired bad person and separate the collection function from the workout function. The third party becomes the power that collects money, rather than leaving the owner hoping that a member will pay the club. A club really doesn't enjoy any leverage for collections.

The issue is: Does EFT have a higher collection rate than people who simply write checks each month to pay their bills? The answer is both yes and no.

Overall, EFT payments are collected at an average rate of about 7 to 8 percent better than checks written each month. It seems logical that this number should be much higher because the club is automatically collecting the payments directly from the member's account each month, but in reality the difference isn't that great. It also seems that it should be higher because the companies that are EFT processors, as opposed to true third-party financial-service companies, claim that by using EFT you will collect all the money from all the members every month.

Unfortunately, no one collects all the money from all the members each month. No one will ever collect all the money from all the members each month. Anyone that claims to do so doesn't understand the concept of basic loss rates.

The illusion of EFT is that it is a magical cure for a club's collection woes. EFT is advertised directly at most clubs' weakest part, the backshop business area. A club owner who has tried ineffective systems is drawn to the magic cure being offered by a system that claims to be so effective in solving the gym owner's biggest headache. These clubs often use EFT as the only method of payment, besides paying cash for the year, setting up an adversarial relationship between a potential member and the club.

According to the major business magazines, only about 50 percent of the people in the country are comfortable with EFT as part of their bill-paying routine. The exceptions are a person's insurances, car payment, and investments, which a slightly higher percentage of people are comfortable using EFT to pay.

Assuming that owners build most of their clubs to appeal to the top 60 percent of the area's demographics, it can probably be estimated that the more financially sophisticated segment of the market is most likely more comfortable with having their accounts automatically drafted. You might then be able to project that at least 60 to 70 percent of your target market is likely to be okay with an EFT system.

That projection still leaves 30 to 40 percent of your market uncomfortable with giving their checking account information or credit card numbers to a club. And if the potential member is not comfortable with giving out that information, then he will most likely not be happy with paying for a membership in full, which is often the only membership alternative a club that forces EFT will give.

Club owners often say, "I have no problem with EFT at my club. Not a single member that enrolled complained about having to use it." In this case, it's not the members who enrolled that are the problem; the problem is the potential members who never even came into the club because they know they have to use EFT.

Paying your rent or mortgage payment is a necessity. Making your car payment is something you just have to do. Joining a club is something a person can do without because they are using discretionary money, which is money left over in their life to do with as they please after they have paid all their other real-life bills.

EFT does have a place in the club business as a method of payment option, but it does not guarantee collections. It just makes collections simpler in some situations, especially if you aren't using a strong third-party collection company in conjunction with your EFT.

Unfortunately, no one collects all the money from all the members each month.

Doing It Yourself

Many people in the gym business are in it because they were such lousy employees in the real world. In other words, they are somewhat unhirable, because gym owners would rather do things themselves than let people tell them what to do.

Collecting your own memberships is the ultimate example of trying to be in control. The problem with this scenario is that the more you try to do yourself, the less control you really have in your business, because of one of the true maxims in the business:

You can manage more than you can do yourself.

Collecting and serving your own memberships usually means higher loss rates, little economy of scale (even if you have multiple units, you seldom get to the point where it is cost effective to establish your own billing and collection company), and higher risk, because your most important asset is controlled and managed by too few people. In other words, if you have three units and a small office set up to service your own accounts managed by two or three people, you are only one car wreck away, especially if these people go to lunch together, from being out of business.

You can collect your own memberships, but the effectiveness is seldom adequate. Generally, two key things go wrong when you service your own accounts. First, your effort is concentrated on the good members that would have paid no matter what you did to them and not enough on the problem members who move, close accounts, are chronically late with their payments, get divorced, are overdrawn on their accounts, or any of the multitude of problems associated with trying to collect payments from hundreds of members. Even with an in-house system that forces EFT as the only membership option, you will still have problems with closed accounts and overdrawn accounts. Remember that no one collects all the money from all the members every time.

The second common issue with do-it-yourself collection systems is that the losses are too big too soon. Remember, the national average for the cost of collection with a major third-party financial service company is approximately 7 percent. This number represents the combination of the charges for the servicing and collection of EFT and the slightly higher charges for the servicing and collection of coupon/check payments.

Owners that collect their own memberships usually do a decent job of servicing and collecting from the members who willingly pay each month. The difficulty arises from the problem members.

Instead of collecting these payments for the 7 percent average, these problem accounts are turned over to an end-of-the-road collection company. Clubs don't normally do well in chasing down and solving member account problems. This work is vastly detailed and it's hard to develop a process that can systematically turn a troubled member account back into a strong, reliable payment.

These companies specialize in hardcore collections on bad accounts and they usually charge somewhere between 33 and 50 percent of what's collected. They can do their job, but the problem is that most of the membership contracts they received as bad accounts would have never been turned over to them in the first place if the club had been using a sophisticated third-party financial-service company.

Third-Party Financial-Service Companies

The name "third-party financial-service company" is in many ways not even a valid name anymore. This type of company has evolved into more of a data-management provider for clubs, since a true third-party company now provides much more to a club than the servicing and collection of member accounts.

The name "third-party" came about because clubs used the illusion of a strong outside company to collect their payments. It didn't take owners long to figure out that the club would be the last thing to get paid each month by the member, since the club had no leverage to collect. What was the club going to do, kick the member out? He already wasn't paying and wanted out anyway.

In essence, data-management companies become your partner in your business by allowing the club to totally concentrate on the production side of the business while the third-party company concentrates on giving you management information and strong cash flow from the memberships the club sells over time. This partnership provides the long-term stability and planning ability a club owner needs to continue to grow a business over the years.

The next step

With the advent of the Internet, the third-party financial-service/data-management companies have evolved another step. The logical course is that all your data will be held, stored, and maintained in the data-management company's computers and you will access all of your account information online.

Of course, problems will surface in the delivery system initially, but over time the club owner should gain quicker access and more pertinent information to make club-management decisions. For example, a club owner might be considering a change in her marketing plan. A few simple key strokes on her computer and she should be able to access the demographics of her current membership, including where they live, ages, usage in the club, income, email address, average member payment, and other information that would influence the type and amount of marketing a club would need to do to establish a niche or specialization. Other information that becomes available to the owner in this scenario would be the amount spent in profit centers during each member visit, renewal percentages, and daily cash flow from all sources.

Factors That Influence the Strength of Your Receivable Base

Four major factors influence the strength of your receivable base and the total money you will collect over time from your membership base. These four factors, when applied to a single payment, determine the yield an owner can expect from an average membership over a year's period of time.

The owner of any fitness business only has one main purpose: to strengthen and protect his most valuable asset, which is the receivable base. All of these factors can be controlled to some extent and an owner needs to do whatever it takes to minimize the effect each has on the club's total outstanding contracts to be collected. These four factors are as follows:

- Loss rate
- Cancellations made by the club
- Cost of collections and servicing member payments
- Free enhancements added as part of the membership

The loss rate

The term "loss rate" can be understood in a number of ways, but the simplest is to think of it as money you should have collected from the members but didn't because they opted not to pay for some reason. For example, assume a club signed up 100 new members in July of last year. True loss rate would mean that you track those 100 members through their year and determine exactly when they stopped paying on their membership agreements.

The club in this example is using 12-month agreements, which should have an annual loss rate of about 10 percent, which means that 10 people will not pay for whatever reason, but 90 will pay until the end of their membership term. This example also assumes that the club is using a strong third-party financial-service company to service these memberships.

Another way to look at this situation is that the club will lose slightly less than 1 percent of its 100 hundred members each month for 12 months. The reasons this scenario gets complicated is that the club is also adding new members every month and other reasons exist why a member may not pay. These reasons are discussed later in this chapter.

"Applied to principle" is another way to consider loss rate. This term means that each month the total outstanding principle to be collected, which is represented by the amount each member has to pay on the remaining balance of his contract with the club (i.e., the obligation), changes. During each month, the club adds new members to its total outstanding, but it also subtracts in the form of members who make their last payment but don't renew, those who elect not to pay, members who have a legitimate reason to suspend payment such as a move or medical reason, and those who pay the balance of their membership in full when it gets down to the last few payments. You can then compare what should have been collected from your total outstanding against what is actually collected each month and figure out the loss.

The club doesn't need to have a true loss rate or the exact amount applied to principle. However, to gain valuable information on protecting and strengthening your receivable base, all you really need is to understand that during each month a certain percentage of contracts will kick out of your system, and then work with this average. Three prime factors directly affect how high or low the loss rate will be:

- The higher the pressure at the point of sale, the higher the loss rate will be
- The loss rate associated with each membership tool the club uses
- Overpromising and underdelivering

High pressure produces high loss rates.

Some people just sign a membership agreement to get away from the salesperson in hopes of getting out of the club alive. Pounding people into submission results in higher loss rates, especially in what's called first-payment defaults. First-payment defaults are people who, after thinking about their sales experience in the club, feel that some slick salesperson talked them into something they didn't really want. They then exact their revenge on the salesperson and the club by defaulting on the first payment on their membership agreement. It doesn't matter if the member writes a check or is set up on EFT, they will find a way to not make that first payment.

Clubs that practice strong first-visit sales closing should track their first-payment defaults, both by the club's total and by individual salesperson. A salesperson who claims an unusually high first-visit closing rate will almost always have the elevated first-payment default number to go along with it.

Normally, a good salesperson in a club will close approximately 30 to 40 percent of their first visits over time. If they are closing at a higher rate, then their first-payment defaults should be tracked monthly.

The key element behind pressure sales is the term "buyer's regret," which means that somebody bought something and then had serious second thoughts immediately after the purchase. For example, you go to the mall to buy sandals and two hours later you're sitting in your living room feeling bad about that entire new outfit you just bought because some salesperson said, "Hey, you really look good in those shorts and they really go well with those sandals you were looking at." This feeling is buyer's regret, or the "What the hell did I buy this time?" feeling you get while thinking of how you are going to pay for this purchase.

In most cases, the club actually causes buyer's regret. Too much emphasis is put on the first visit. In addition, the use of discounts at the point of sale both adds to high buyer's regret and makes losses higher than they need to be.

Trial memberships take a lot of the buyer's regret out of the picture because the consumer has an actual chance to try before he buys. With trials, the consumer also feels that he is in more control of the buying situation than he does when forced to make a buying decision 20 minutes after visiting a club for the first time.

True trial memberships, coupled with a strong third-party financial-service company and 12-month contracts, can usually drop a club's loss rate to less than 10 percent annually. Most of this gain occurs because the client felt he actually participated in the buying decision instead of being forced into something he didn't even know he really wanted when he decided to check out a gym on the way home from work.

The tool the club uses influences the loss rate.

Who collects and how the memberships are collected are factors in how much money the club will collect from its memberships through its receivable base. Using a strong third-party financial-service company will significantly increase the overall money you collect from your memberships.

The tool you use with the members also plays a role in how collectable your membership agreements are. "Tool" is defined as the agreement and term the club uses to define its relationship with its members. For example, one club might use a 12-month membership agreement, another may use a 24-month agreement, and a third in the same area might use month-to-month, pay-as-you-go memberships. Each tool has its positives and negatives regarding its effect on the club's loss rate.

This month-to-month, pay-as-you-go tool was popularized by some of the chain clubs. This type of membership means that the club does not establish any type of obligation with the member. The member can simply pay month-to-month and cancel any time he chooses. Members love this option, but it is not the best tool to stabilize a business because the losses are so high.

This type of membership seemed to be a knee-jerk reaction to the clubs that forced long-term memberships upon their members and then suffered the wrath of State Attorney Generals all over the country. Instead of contracts, why not just let the members pay month-to-month and come and go as they please?

Several problems exist for a club with this type of membership. The losses are approximately 3 to 4 percent per month at the very least, or about 36 to 48 percent annually. If a club signs up 100 members in January, by the end of December it will only have between 52 and 64 of those members left. In other words, you could lose half your members over time, just through the loss rates associated with this type of membership.

This type of membership seems logical, but is actually not a good thing for the club. Clubs using month-to-month memberships have to do the same work to sign up a new member a club using a fixed obligation does, run the same if not more marketing because the losses are so high, and have the same start-up cost per new member and the same labor cost to get the new member into the system. In other words, they have the same costs, but much less of a chance to collect money from the membership over a year's period of time.

Month-to-month memberships may work in very high-volume markets such as San Francisco or Manhattan, but owners in the rest of the country should be careful using month-to-month memberships because of the excessive loss rates.

The recommendation to avoid using month-to-month memberships has an exception. Club owners that feel they need to compete with other clubs in their market that feature month-to-month options can offer the same tool but in a different format. This type of club would offer month-to-month memberships at a rate of about $8 to $10 more per month than its 12-month contract rate. Given a choice, approximately 80 percent of the members will chose a 12-month option if it is priced $10 lower than the month-to-month option. If the member wants the freedom to truly come and go, then he can choose that option. If, on the other hand, he intends to support the club year-round, he can then save approximately $120 per year by choosing the annual membership.

For example, if the club sold 12-month memberships for $49 per month, it could offer a month-to-month option for $57 to 59 per month, coupled with a slightly larger membership fee. Using the $8 to $10 spread, approximately 80 percent of the club's new members each month should take the 12-month membership, which provides more stability and lower losses than the month-to-month memberships, thereby giving the club a higher return per member.

Overpromising and underdelivering

Salespeople that promise more than the club can deliver also drive up the loss rate for the club. This statement is especially true for a club sales team that promises a lot of free help for the new member to get started and then the trainers, or even the salespeople if they are the ones who have to deliver the workouts, are always too busy and the workouts are short and poor in quality.

General customer service is also an issue. If the new member is promised great service but can't get a towel during her first visit, has to wait to get on a cardio machine, or can't get into a class that is too full, she will take it out on the club by not paying or canceling her membership. Members don't mind paying when they get what they pay for, but they will fight if the promised service is not delivered.

Promise only what you can deliver and don't create scenarios based upon service the club doesn't have the staff or training to deliver. Most losses in this category are preventable, but club owners with aggressive sales staff have to be particularly on guard to prevent a high-pressure salesperson from guaranteeing something the club can't back up.

Cancellations made by the club

Your cancellation policy should be restricted to only what the law allows in your state. Typical state cancellation policies are usually pretty simple and very straightforward. For example, most states require that you cancel the membership of anyone who moves more than 25 miles away from the club.

Most club managers, however, too easily cancel someone who moves instead of following a set policy that reflects a combination of common sense and the state law as it reads. This simple law is made much too complicated by many club owners. The tough part comes when you try to verify the move, especially when you don't have a predetermined policy in place.

A bad scenario takes place when a young female or a drinking buddy comes into the club and says, "I'm moving and need to cancel." Your young manager, either interested in the young female or going drinking with the friend that night, and lacking a policy to follow, says, "Sure, I'll take care of that." The membership is cancelled and the club loses a chance to collect the remainder of the contract, revenue that had cost the club a commission to sell as well as marketing expense and set-up costs for the new member.

Two issues are in play in this situation. The club should farm out its cancellations during your first year of business. If you pick a solid, third-party financial-service company, they will be able to set up your cancellations in your club's file.

In this example, the manager should have said, "We actually don't handle the cancellations here at the club. Please call this 800 number and our service company will help you." The service company would then cancel per your instructions and per your state laws. A typical response might be, "Your club and state will allow the cancellation of your membership if you move more than 25 miles away from the club. Please send a copy of your new utility bill once you arrive and you will be cancelled immediately."

Utility bills are the hardest to fake and are good tools to keep the members honest. Again, this situation could have been handled by the service company or by the club itself if it had the right systems in place. If you handle it at the club level, you then have a chance to try and resign the member and get him or her back in the club again, especially since a large number of these casual cancellations are nothing more than members who simply aren't using the club at the time.

Your goal is to keep your cancellations to 1 percent of your total file each month. For example, if you have 1200 members, you should only have 12 or fewer that actually move more than 25 miles or cancel for other legitimate reasons, such as permanent medical disability. Loose managers that are too easy and don't understand the laws of the state they live in can easily hit 3 percent per month in cancellations. Check this number monthly once you open and work hard to keep it near 1 percent.

This example assumes that you are using membership contracts. Month-to-month, pay-as-you-go memberships allow most members to cancel with 30 days notice, which means that your cancellations will be included in your overall loss rates associated with the tool you select for memberships, which was discussed earlier in this chapter. In the case of open-ended memberships, the losses will be at least 3 to 4 percent per month and probably higher.

Some states also allow for a cancellation fee. Remember, cancellation fees are not another profit center, as in, "Hey, we made $200 in cancellation fees today. Yahoo." You had to cancel part of your receivable base to generate those fees and you gave up part of your future to collect a small percentage of what was owed you in total membership dollars. Again, if your state allows you to charge a fee to cancel, and you have a legitimate cancellation, then go for the money. Learn to fight for every dollar and make sure you try to save every member who is trying to leave the club.

Cost of collections and servicing member payments

The national average for the cost of collections using a third-party financial-service company is about 7 percent of what is collected. And no, you can't beat that number and efficiently collect your own memberships. Are you getting into the business to build a financially successful fitness business dedicated to helping members and providing a legendary service experience or are you getting into the business so you can chase people for missed payments?

Remember the foundational rule of any small business: If it gets in the way of production, farm it out. Do not do your own payroll, because it gets in the way of generating new revenue. Don't do our own accounting, except for basic QuickBooks®, since it gets in the way of producing new money every day. And don't do your own servicing of your members, because your time is better spent generating new memberships and letting a professional company collect the most money from the most members possible.

You will have extra cost associated with your service company. Some companies charge separately for software and some have extra services available in a menu-driven format, letting you choose the tools that fit your new business. Some companies offer other support tools, such as lead-generation tools, that you might pay extra for if you can use them for your business. Check the cost first and then choose the items you need to be successful.

Also, remember that it is always cheaper to buy proven tools off the shelf than to try to copy and recreate everything because you're cheap. Do it right and use proven tools and always concentrate on the production end of the business as your first priority.

Free enhancements added as part of the membership

Everything has a cost and that cost has to be absorbed into the business somehow. The best example is the owner who likes to give out free coffee in the morning, thinking that he is providing great customer service. The coffee is cheap and the cups are small, and yet he ends up spending approximately $770 to $900 per month to provide an unnecessary and wasteful service.

Customer service is never free. Instead of being wasteful, you should offer quality options. This same club owner could offer quality coffee in 16 to 20 ounce cups for

$1.50, along with a special flavored coffee of the week, and thrill his members. If the coffee is good, reasonably priced, and convenient, the club will make some profit while providing excellent customer service.

Watch for the money-losing traps, because these money wasters lower the overall return per member in your business. For example, if an owner also gave out free towels and free childcare, it would cost him about two dollars per month per member in most clubs, which is a lot of money. In addition, he has to lower the value of these items because he is losing money on each of them every time the member uses one of these services.

Get a good coffee bar and build a legendary childcare room and then charge for it. The towels, especially if you are in a club that charges $49 per month or higher, are something you include for free. But if you are in a club that charges less, offer nice towels and charge customers one dollar to use them.

Most new owners try to give everything away, thinking it will drive their business, but you'll find that it is hard to maintain quality when giving things away for free. Free childcare almost always comes down to a small room with badly painted walls, a cheap television, and lousy toys. If you're going to offer something, do it well and then charge for the extra quality you are offering the members. Keep in mind that the member will pay for nice things, but you usually can't give cheap stuff away.

Your goal is to hit zero. In other words, you want to eliminate as many things that lower your return per member as you can and replace them with offerings that the members will pay to support.

You want to eliminate as many things that lower your return per member as you can and replace them with offerings that the members will pay to support.

Building a Membership Structure

This section provides basic information that you can use to start your thinking process. More information about building an effective structure can be found in other Thomas Plummer books and seminars, but this example will help you build your first business plan.

The core of the membership system is the 12-month membership coupled with a one-time membership fee. New members would pay the one-time fee immediately, and their first payment would be due about 30 days from the day they sign the contract. For example:

$69 one-time fee + $59 a month (EFT) for 12 months

The one-time membership fee should be at least equal to one month's dues, but no more than $89 for most clubs. Exceptions exist to that rule, but most clubs will benefit by having at least one membership where someone can start for $89 or less.

Do not get the first month's dues and the membership fee together. The combination of the two would make it over $89 per month, thus limiting your ability to get the consumer to make an impulse buy. This scenario is called payment in arrears, and it allows the club owner to build a stronger receivable base because he is getting 12 payments rather than 11. For example, the money could arrive as follows:

- Today's date is November 15, 2006.
- A member who joins today would put down $69 as the one-time membership fee.
- The date the membership begins is November 15, 2006.
- The date of the first payment is December 15, 2006, and the payment amount is $59.
- The date the membership expires is November 15, 2007 (not December 15, 2007) and the final payment of $59 is due that day.

Again, you should always offer the person the choice of writing a check each month. Using EFT is becoming more popular each year, but you still should not force EFT in your club. Give the new member the option to pay a little more to write a check each month (sent to your third-party financial-service company), since you as an owner are usually charged more for processing those checks (Figure 8-2). For example:

$69 one-time fee—$59 a month (EFT) for 12 months
or
$69 one-time fee—$64 a month (coupon/check system) for 12 months

2005 Club Membership Prices by Club Type and Club Size All Clubs				
	Enrollment/Initiation Fee		Monthly Dues	
	Median	Middle Range	Median	Middle Range
Regular individual (single adult)	$150.00	$99.00–$300.00	$53.48	$43.08–$77.7
Corporate individual	$92.71	$50.00–$206.25	$47.00	$37.00–$66.00
Couple	$199.50	$99.00–$490.00	$88.00	$61.75–$127.13
Family	$200.00	$99.00–$450.00	$104.00	$70.00–$156.00
Junior	$99.00	$50.00–$175.00	$39.00	$30.00–$49.00
Senior citizen	$100.00	$68.03–$245.00	$44.00	$35.00–$56.71

Data from a sample of IHRSA North American Health Clubs. *Profiles of Success*, 2006.

Figure 8-2. Examples of additional club prices

Markets with competitors using open-ended memberships

If you are in an area that has a lot of competitors using the open-ended, month-to-month, pay-as-you-go option, you need to show one as well. That membership offering should cost at least $8 to $10 higher than your regular annual membership. It may seem like you will get less from your annuals, but you will collect more money from more members over time due to the lower loss rates as compared to those seen with open-ended memberships For example:

$69 membership fee—$69 per month open-ended, pay-as-you-go
or
$69 membership fee—$59 a month for 12 months

Price-sensitive markets

If you are in a price sensitive market, you might show a lower price for a longer commitment to stay competitive without destroying your higher pricing model. For example:

$69 membership fee—$59 a month for 12 months
or
$69 membership fee—$49 a month for 18 months

The 18-month membership is a better choice in most markets than the 24-month membership because of loss rates. The 18-month option usually has loss rates closer to the 12-month membership, or about 1 percent per month, while the 24-month will often have much higher loss rates in the 3 to 4 percent per-month range.

The proper term for two people joining your club together is not "couple rate." The correct term that avoids discrimination is "two people living at the same address." If you offer this type of membership, don't discount severely for two people joining at the same time. A good model is discounting only $5 or so for the second person. You are also better off writing up two separate memberships and getting each individual's personal financial information. Many people keep their own accounts in a relationship and you will collect more money over time by getting separate memberships at the point of sale.

Short-term memberships (good for up to three months)

Avoid junk memberships or too many options. The short-term membership combines many of the shorter options clubs tend to develop over time. A short-term membership should be good for up to three months, and has to be paid all at once. If the consumer bought four of them (totaling one year), he should end up paying approximately $200 more than your regular membership. For example, you could use the following pricing structure:

- Standard membership: $69 + ($59 x 12) = $777
- $777 + $200 = $977
- $977/4 = $244 (round up to $249) for a three-month membership.

Daily fees

Your daily drop-in fee should be at least $15 to 20 in most markets and higher where you can get it. Have a high daily fee, because you want to be able to offer a member's guest a deal, which is usually half the daily fee. If you don't have this option in place, the members often expect you to let their guests in for free. This scenario allows you to still get paid, but the member and his guest are both happy as well. For example, if your daily fee is $15, the member's guest would pay $7.50.

If you have a large percentage of transient guests, such as professionals visiting the area for short periods of time, consider a punch card. For example, you can offer a punch card at a price of 10 visits for $99 to $120 (based upon a daily fee of $15). Put a two-month expiration on these cards.

VIP and other membership options

If you live in a resort area, don't cheapen the week by selling it cheaply. A better way is to call it the VIP week and offer a T-shirt, a full seven days of workouts, a few bottles of water, and maybe some tanning. Price this package at approximately $69 for the week, but don't forget: If you're on vacation, it's all about bringing home the cool shirt.

Many clubs, especially those are catering to an upscale or older market, are doing away with discounting for older members. Keep in mind that as the population continues to age, at some point most of your members would qualify for the senior discount. Consider going without this discount if you can.

Most clubs are also moving away from discounting for cash. Your receivable base is the club's most important asset and you want to do everything you can to grow it as large and as strong as possible. The more effective way to offer a paid-in-full incentive to a potential member who asks is to enhance rather than discount. You can do this by adding several months to the membership (14 for the price of 12 for example) instead of cutting the cost. The club still gets full price, but most importantly, all the members are paying the same price, which protects your integrity in the market.

Sample Price Structure

Standard option:
$69–$59 x 12 months (EFT)
$69–$64 x 12 months (coupon/check system)

If you have strong open-ended competition, add:
$69–$69 per month, open-ended, pay-as-you-go membership

If you have strong, low-priced competition, add:
$69–$49 x 18 months

Second person at same household:
$89–$99 x 12 (split into two contracts if possible)

Paid-in-full membership:
Add two months, but don't discount for cash

Short-term membership (good for up to three months):
$249 (do not finance/paid all at once)

Daily fees:
$15 to $20 per daily visit

Member/guest:
Half of daily fee for a member's guest who is not qualified for a trial

Punch cards:
10 visits at $99 to $120 (add a two-month expiration to the back)

VIP week:
One full week at $69 to 99, including a T-shirt and assorted stuff

The Key Concept in This Chapter

Your receivable base is everything in your new business. As you conceptualize your business, always start with the financial foundation, which is how the member pays, how much he pays, and who collects the money each month. If you get these things right, you can make a lot of mistakes and stay in business. Get these things wrong and you will find that it is hard to sell your way out of trouble.

Most club owners also make the initial mistake of trying to offer membership options that please everyone, which is a bad habit to get into if you want to be profitable. Remember the old adage:

- Rule 1: The customer is always right
- Rule 2: See rule 1

What most people don't know is that the guy who wrote this adage went out of business about 20 minutes after he hung it on the wall. The customer is right many times, especially when the club team makes a mistake, such as incorrect billing or missed appointments, which the club has to correct immediately. But the member/customer is also wrong in many cases, and he often complains simply because he wants to work the system and take advantage of the club. Pricing is the area where club owners get worked the hardest and the pressure is to do whatever it takes to get someone into the system. But if an exception for one person is not offered to everyone, then your reputation and integrity are damaged and that will cost you a lot more money in the future than holding the line with members who want memberships designed just for them and won't join unless they get that special deal.

Successful pricing and membership collection should be fair to both sides. The members should have a number of membership options offered fairly to everyone and the club should have a system in place that allows it to collect the most money from the most members that is legally and ethically possible. If both sides win, then the business will endure and the club owner will make the most money he can in that market.

Additional Resource

IHRSA's Profiles of Success, 2006
    www.ihrsastore.com

9

Staffing

Staffing will be the hardest issue you deal with in your new fitness career and your success will be defined in the future by your ability to find, develop, and motivate your staff to drive revenue in your business and to provide legendary customer service. When you first open your new business, you will have to build systems that can be carried out by a variety of people as your staff comes and goes through the first year. Some people will stick with you and be loyal over time, while others will simply pass through the business and end up leaving you at what seems like all the worst times.

Building Systems From the Start

Systems can be defined as set procedures that are available in writing for each employee to learn and follow so that he can do any job required of him in your new business. When you hire someone new, all training is done through the set procedures for the area of the club where that person will work.

Your training will be easier, and you will make more money, if you develop a procedure manual for your business before you even open. Procedure manuals are simple notebooks that have each action an employee would do in his department clearly explained in less than two pages.

Sample pages for your manual might include:

- How to fill out a membership agreement correctly, with a sample of one that is well done and one that might show common errors circled in red
- How to open the club
- How to close the club at the end of the day
- How to troubleshoot the front-counter computers
- How to answer the phone, including sample scripts

Each one of these procedures should be in defined and written in the simplest and most straightforward of terms. For example, consider a situation in which you are not at the club and the front-counter computer isn't working. The employee would grab the manual, turn to the troubleshooting computer page, and read the following:

- Is the computer plugged in? Yes or no?
- Is the computer turned on? Yes or no?
- Are other things that are plugged in on the counter also not working?
- If other things are not working, go to the breaker box, which located in the hall closet and marked "Breaker Box" in large letters on the front.
- Find the switch marked "Front Counter."
- Flip the switch once to the left and then hard to the right.

Developing procedure manuals early in the process makes your training much easier. You simply turn to the section for the department the person is working in and go through all of the key procedures he might encounter as the fundamentals for that position. In the training department, for example, a new trainer might spend the first few hours of the first day of training going through pages covering the following topics:

- Your training philosophy
- What is expected of a trainer
- Dress codes for trainers
- How to meet, greet, and handle a client
- Selling a member on more sessions
- Meeting new members in the club

Each one of these topics would be covered in less than a page. The most important thing, however, is that everyone who starts in that department begins with the same basic knowledge, understands the fundamentals of that job, and knows where to look first if they have any questions.

Your training will be easier, and you will make more money, if you develop a procedure manual for your business before you even open.

Establishing a Common Sales Language

It is very important to have all of your employees explaining everything in your business the same way each and every time. When you first open, things will be wild, but you want to be sure that every new member hears the same information about your offerings, services, and programming.

A simple tool to help employees master a common sales language from the start is the 4 x 5 card stack. This low-tech training tool consists of nothing more than a stack of index cards. On the front of each card is just one service, product, class, or customer-service issue. On the back are three benefits or responses necessary to explain the item on the front. For example:

The front:

Cycle classes

The back:

Low-impact cardio
All the energy, excitement, and craziness of being in a small group
Everyone can ride at his own level and still get the best cardio workout in the club

Each employee would start with a stack of these cards the day they are hired. If you have a few minutes to train someone, just grab their cards and read the front of one and test that person on their knowledge of the back. This technique allows you to spot coach as well if the new hire doesn't understand that product or service.

When you first open the club, you might have a small stack of cards, but as you progress through your first 90 days, keep adding to everyone's pile. It is important to develop a consistent sales talk in the club, as inconsistent messages are the easiest way to irritate your members when it comes to customer service.

Building a Team

At some point, you have to develop a team that can take responsibility for their own areas of the business. Most new owners, however, are slow to do this because they spend far too much time trying to do everything themselves.

If you have a small club, you will obviously end up carrying much more of the load yourself. As your club grows in size, your chances for success will be better if you can build a team of people who are responsible for the revenue in the key areas of the club.

A variety of management models are seen in the club business, but most fall into one of three classifications. The only one that will get you to the highest level of financial success, though, is the third one. Study these models carefully and try to build that team early.

Working *in* your business, not *on* your business

O = owner
T = team members

TTTTTTTOTTTTTT

In this first model, the owner simply takes a job in his own club. This model is most common among trainers, who are known as technicians. A trainer might start off with a small club where he trains almost every client. At some point, he decides to build something larger, where he still trains most of the clients.

The least effective thing you can do in your own club is train members. You manage, you sell memberships, you develop staff, your greet people at the desk, and take care of customer service, but you don't need to be training clients. Most owners using this model all say the same thing: "I am the best trainer and they will all leave if I don't train them." Yes, you might lose a few, but over time your business will grow if you spend those hours training the other trainers and the rest of your staff.

Batman and Robin

O = owner
S = sidekick
T = team members

O (Batman)
S (Robin)
TTTTTTTTTTTTTTTTT

In this second model, you do most of the work and then when you get to the point where you can't get everything done, you hire a sidekick to do all the tasks that you don't want to do anymore. The limitation of this model is that you can never grow the business past your personal workload. Notice that every employee answers directly to the owner, which means that no one does anything unless you tell him what to do. The other big issue is, what happens when Robin quits? You don't have systems in this model; you have simply tried to split yourself into two people.

The preferred model

O = owner
M = managers
T = team members

O
M M M M
TTTTTTTTTTTTT

The preferred model is to hire people who are in charge of the key revenue areas in the club and then spend your day working with them and helping them reach their numbers with their teams. In this model, the owner oversees the managers, who oversee the team members.

The Key Positions in Your New Business

When you build your new management structure, start with the key areas of revenue and get someone in charge of those areas. Small clubs will have a smaller version of this system, but you must have someone take individual responsibility for the key areas of any business of any size.

A common mistake in most clubs is that too many people are on the operations side and not enough people are given the accountability and responsibility for production. In the fitness business, 95 percent of the job is production and 5 percent is operations. In other words, the main role for most staff in a gym business is to sell somebody something every day.

The main role for most staff in a gym business is to sell somebody something every day.

The following jobs are the key roles in most clubs. Note that the major areas where you will make money, such as sales, training, and nutrition, all have dedicated people who are responsible for the total production of that department.

Manager

The manager, who works 45 to 50 hours per week, has two focuses. He handles the operational part of the business, such as budgeting and staffing, while also supervising and participating in the production side of the business. Most importantly, the manager is responsible for the club's total revenues.

The manager's role in operations is as follows:

- Hiring, developing, coaching, and firing staff
- Daily reporting and number analysis
- Advertising
- Budgets and budgeting
- Working the club during prime revenue hours

The manager's role in production is as follows:

- Selling memberships
  - 50 percent of all sales in clubs with under 600 members
  - 10 to 20 percent of all sales in larger clubs
- Driving the revenues through actions plans
- Budgeting and planning events
- Driving the revenues through sales and promotion of the club's profit centers

Sales manager

This person, who works 45 to 50 hours per week, has one function: Get the total number of membership sales needed each month. Even small training centers and small women-only clubs have to have one person in charge of member acquisition. If your sales come together, the rest of the club will have a better chance of succeeding.

The sales manager should:

- Sell between 40 and 50 percent of the club's sales
- Provide daily training for the sales team and hold the daily meeting
- Train the entire staff on sales at least once a month
- Manage the club's electronic marketing and all follow-up of the club's prospective members

Lead counter person

The lead counter person, works 32 to 45 hours per week, is in many ways the most important person in the club, since he is your lead person at the front-counter area during the business's prime time. This person also supervises the rest of the front-desk personnel, as well as drives the club's profit centers, including drinks, shakes, and supplement sales, which might be housed in the front-counter area.

The lead counter person should:

- Train and supervise all counter people
- Be in the club during prime time Monday through Thursday night, because the members seek consistency
- Meet, greet, and handle all potential members during prime time
- Assist in the promotion and revenue production of the club's profit centers during his shift

Weekend supervisor

This entry-level management job, which requires 45 hours of work per week, allows the club to have a management-team member on duty during the prime production hours on Saturday morning. This person's schedule could be structured in several different ways over a three- or four-day span.

The weekend supervisor should:

- Open and close the club on Saturday
- Close the club on Sundays
- Be off every fifth weekend
- Be in charge of the weekend production, including selling memberships and promoting profit centers
- Work the rest of their hours in the club early in the week as a regular staff person

Lead nutrition professional

This person, who works between 32 and 45 hours per week, is the liaison between your club and your nutrition/weight-loss management company. This profit center is so important that one person should be dedicated to driving the revenues from this area.

The nutrition professional should:

- Work with the weight-loss management company to drive the revenues from this area

- Educate the members and promote supplements in the club
- Educate and train the training staff on supplements

Lead sports activity/conditioning professional (formerly called the head trainer)

This person, who works 32 to 50 hours per week, is responsible for driving revenues in the personal training and semi-private group-training areas in the club.

The lead sports activity/conditioning professional should:

- Acquire and develop trainers in the club
- Write protocol and then supervise the training department
- Train staff and then develop supplement sales in the training department
- Be responsible for all revenue in the sports activity/conditioning department

The group exercise director

This person, who works 20 to 45 hours per week, is responsible for driving the numbers in the group-exercise department. This person's ultimate goal is to get 30 to 40 percent of the club's daily traffic into some form of group exercise. This person does not have to be an instructor. Anyone who loves group exercise, such as a salesperson or trainer, can be the director if they have a little business sense.

The group exercise director should:

- Attend a national group exercise director management-training workshop. These types of workshops can be found in IHRSA's associate member listing.
- Do scheduling and class analysis for profitability for the entire program
- Train and develop nontraditional instructors
- Complete roll-out and promotion of each of the club's offerings in the group-exercise department

When to Hire Your New Team

Do not hire your team and put them on the payroll until you have a definite opening date for your business. Owners that hire too soon, and too far in advance, will often lose money or staff if the club is delayed for whatever reason, and it will most likely be delayed.

A rule that covers this very common phenomenon is called the Plummer 20/20 rule. This rules states that your new club will be 20 percent over budget and open at least

20 percent later than you planned. It's like building your own house. You see a tile that wasn't in your budget and you can't live without it, but hey, it's only a $1,000 more. After a few months, you are really over budget because those $1,000 hits add up over time.

Clubs also seldom open on time for a variety of reasons, most of which are out of your control. Strikes, landlord issues, building permits, builders that can't handle the job, late additions or subtractions to the plans, and just bad luck all add up to not opening when you thought you would.

Few clubs open on time and even fewer open within budget, so be prepared and understand what you are getting into with this new project. Adhere to the following guidelines when hiring your team:

- Get your managers in place approximately 45 days out but leave them in their current jobs until two weeks out.

- Your first hire is always going to be a salesperson. Get someone on the team that can generate new memberships from the presale forward.

- Concentrate on production and farm out the rest. Your presale time and the first 90 days of your new business are extremely important. Anything that gets in the way of generating revenue, such as trying to do payroll or collect your own memberships, needs to be handed out to the professionals. Your job is to expand the business, and that's where you need to focus.

- Get your entire team hired and on the payroll simultaneously two weeks out and start intense training. Follow the same steps a new member, and potential member, would go through in your business. For example, what will you give the potential member to take home if they become a new member? What will he take if he doesn't become a member? How will you answer the phone and greet people at the counter? Who has learned the software and can all the counter people use it effectively? Train for all the expected combinations. If you can get into your club before you open, try and train in the actual areas.

- Just a few people can usually handle presale. See Chapter 11 for more information.

- Set your new employees up to be paid twice a month, never every other week. If you do every other week, you will end up with two months a year with triple payrolls, which plays badly on your budgeting and cash flow.

- Get employee manuals in place before you open. Look at the resources at the end of this book if you don't have a source for these tools.

- Become a member of IHRSA and get their information on hiring and firing. Every employee, including childcare providers and janitors, should sign a nonsolicitation agreement.

- During your first month of operation, try and meet with your team at least once a day and problem-solve. Issues will arise concerning such things as customer service, which need to be addressed and handled early.

IHRSA can give you some guidance regarding what people earn in clubs similar to your new project (Figure 9-1). These numbers are a solid starting point and can be used in conjunction with the other ideas presented in this and other Thomas Plummer books.

Your Role in Your Own Business

Learn to sell. If this is your first fitness business, learn to ethically sell memberships, and other services and products, in your business. During your first 90 days, personally sell as many memberships as you can. This practice will make it easier in the future to hire and train the sales staff, because you will have experience.

Your overall job is to drive revenue and keep your managers on track to hit their numbers. The important thing to remember is that you have to have a plan every day to make money. How much are you targeting today and how will you and your team make this money?

The day you open you need to start having a daily meeting to drive revenue. Keeping your staff focused on what has to happen each day is probably the single most important thing you do as an owner/operator. Follow these guidelines in your daily meeting:

It must be held daily:

- Hold the meeting between 12:00 and 4:00. Make it the same time every day and never miss a day.

All full-time department heads must attend:

- A separate meeting should be held for the salespeople.

Keep it to less than half an hour:

- Keep it positive and focused.
- Discuss how much money or how many sales are you going to make between now and tomorrow's meeting.
- No one leaves without a clear understanding of the number their department needs to hit and how they are going to make that number happen.

Set goals for the next 24 hours:

- Set goals for the week and goals that are broken down for the month.

	2004	2005	2006	% Change 2004 to 2005	% Change 2005 to 2006
Senior Management/Corporate Staff					
Chief Executive Officer	$99,750	$82,250	$112,500	-17.50%	36.80%
Chief Operating Officer	$81,800	$91,000	$91,000	11.20%	0.00%
Chief Financial Officer	$75,000	$90,000	$95,000	20.00%	5.60%
Regional Club Manager	$80,000	$70,000	$100,000	-12.50%	42.90%
Sales & Marketing	$49,960	$45,513	$60,500	-8.90%	32.90%
Information Systems	$51,730	$60,000	$68,675	16.00%	14.50%
Human Resources	$41,640	$45,000	$55,250	8.10%	22.80%
Fitness	$47,250	$40,000	$45,609	-15.30%	14.00%
Legal Affairs	**	$59,500	*	**	*
Development	$88,594	$50,000	$106,000	-43.60%	112.00%
Accounting	$38,000	$40,975	$42,000	7.80%	2.50%
Salaried Club-Level Employees					
General Manager	$57,200	$64,960	$66,899	13.60%	3.00%
Sales/Marketing Director	$42,000	$42,100	$45,000	0.20%	6.90%
Sales Representative	$31,600	$32,000	$33,300	1.30%	4.10%
Fitness Director	$39,000	$40,000	$45,000	2.60%	12.50%
Group Exercise/Aerobics Director	$29,600	$30,000	$27,000	1.40%	-10.00%
Tennis Director	$55,000	$65,500	$63,500	19.10%	-3.10%
Assistant General Manager	$38,700	$43,141	$49,600	11.50%	15.00%
Manager on Duty (Shift Director)	$25,000	$27,000	$25,000	8.00%	-7.40%
Athletics or Program Manager	$37,500	$35,000	$35,500	-6.70%	1.40%
Controller or Business Manager	$45,700	$49,000	$45,000	7.20%	-8.20%
Service Manager	$32,500	$31,533	*	-3.00%	*
Office Manager	$33,200	$31,000	$34,500	-6.60%	11.30%
Front-Desk Manager	$27,005	$27,000	$27,000	0.00%	0.00%
Aquatics	$31,000	$30,000	$32,500	-3.20%	8.30%
Food & Beverage Manager	$35,000	$36,000	*	2.90%	*
Children's Programs Manager	$30,000	$31,831	$30,500	6.10%	-4.20%
Pro Shop Manager	$28,844	$34,000	*	17.90%	*%
Maintenance or Housekeeping Manager	$38,000	$36,225	**	-4.70%	**
Maintenance Manager	**	**	$37,000	**	**
Housekeeping Manager	**	**	$30,325	**	**
Summer Camp Director (Full-Time)	$27,200	$29,500	*	8.50%	*%
Childcare Manager	$23,050	$21,120	$21,120	-8.40%	0.00%
Spa Director	**	$30,000	$46,333	**	54.40%
Nutrition/Wellness Director	**	$37,566	$39,240	**	4.50%
Information Systems Director	**	$35,000	$36,000	**	2.90%
Member Service Director	**	$38,500	$36,000	**	-6.50%

* Insufficient data
** Job/position was not reported in this year

Compensation data from IHRSA's survey of North American health clubs; IHRSA's Employee Compensation & Benefits Report, 2006

Figure 9-1. Compensation trends, 2004 to 2006

	2004	2005	2006	% Change 2004 to 2005	% Change 2005 to 2006
Hourly Club-Level Employees (Full-Time)					
Aquatics Instructor	$13.44	$14.00	$14.00	4.20%	0.00%
Personal Trainer	$20.00	$24.00	$23.50	20.00%	-2.10%
Fitness Center Personnel/Instructor	$10.00	$10.00	$10.08	0.00%	0.80%
Tennis Instructor	$25.00	$25.00	$30.00	0.00%	20.00%
Racquetball Instructor	$15.00	*	*	*	*
Group Exercise/Aerobic Instructor	$21.83	$22.00	$23.76	0.80%	8.00%
Pilates Instructor	$26.00	$25.00	$30.00	-3.80%	20.00%
Yoga Instructor	$25.00	$25.00	$30.00	0.00%	20.00%
Martial Arts Instructor	$21.00	$24.00	$25.00	14.30%	4.20%
Group Cycling Instructor	$20.00	$20.00	$22.00	0.00%	10.00%
Front-Desk Personnel	$9.00	$9.00	$10.00	0.00%	11.10%
Bookkeeper	$15.00	$14.00	$15.87	-6.70%	13.40%
Office Staff (Admin. or Clerical)	$12.00	$12.65	$13.00	5.40%	2.80%
Maintenance & Housekeeping	$10.00	$10.00	*	0.00%	*
Maintenance	**	**	$12.75	**	**
Housekeeping	**	**	$9.75	**	**
Childcare Staff	$8.00	$8.00	$8.62	0.00%	7.70%
Food & Beverage Staff	$9.00	$10.00	$9.50	11.10%	-5.00%
Pro-Shop Staff	$9.00	$10.00	$10.00	11.10%	0.00%
Summer Camp Staff	$8.50	$8.00	$8.78	-5.90%	9.70%

* Insufficient data
** Job/position was not reported in this year

Compensation data from IHRSA's survey of North American health clubs; IHRSA's Employee Compensation & Benefits Report, 2006

- Adjust goals for the heavier-volume days and reduce goals for the lesser days.

Get to the point where no one works without a production goal:

- The owner/general manager should generate his own goals.
- The general manager generates goals for the department heads.
- The department heads generate goals for their teams.
- The manager, in smaller clubs, should generate plans for everyone if needed.

Use a performance contracts:

- You will get more from your employees if you transfer ownership of the work that is going to be done to the person responsible for the work.

Reward excessive success:

- Pay does not have to be fair. If someone is a strong achiever, he needs to get more for his work and get better side bonuses and rewards.

Punish failure:

- If an employee is not hitting goals, he needs to go away. One of the biggest mistakes an owner makes is carrying an employee too long after he stops producing.

Coach (teach) daily:

- Understand the difference between training and teaching.
- Coaching must take place every day, every hour that you are in the business.

You have to have a plan to make money every day:

- Money in the fitness business is made daily, and therefore should be planned daily. Money that is not planned becomes random and will always be less than planned money.

You have to understand where your money comes from in the business. Remember, you can control your revenue to a certain extent by keeping your team leaders focused on what they have to accomplish each day.

The Role of Partners

Partnerships usually work fine until the doors are open. When the reality of the business sets in, most partnerships fail.

Each partner in your business should clearly, and in writing, state what he will do in the new business and what he is responsible for each day. Anger surfaces when two people think they are managing staff, for example, or when one partner realizes that he is carrying the load for the entire club and the other person is just training clients all day.

You also need to clearly and legally define your partnership before you pool money and resources. Your attorney should help you develop a partnership/management agreement before you get too for into the new business. Ask your attorney to cover these issues:

- What happens when someone wants out?
- How do you agree to disagree?
- What if a partner dies or gets divorced?
- What happens if you need to put more money in and one partner doesn't have his share?
- What happens if you want to open another club? Does every partner automatically have the right to be in the new business?
- One partner should have the final decision-making ability to run the business. Who is that in your partnership?
- How do the partners get paid and take money out of the business?
- Who manages the staff (only one person can do so)?

Other issues will be addressed by your attorney, but you need to discuss these valid points with your business partners before you get very far into the deal. It is especially important that you come up with a way to buy out unhappy partners before the business gets going. Unhappy partners often want lots of money because it was their "concept," and although it's not making money at the moment, it will in the future. You can't pay for future money, so keep it clean and define escape clauses up front so that no surprises occur.

Final Thoughts About Your Staffing Efforts

To be successful in the future, you have to move toward an older, more mature, and more productive staff that matches the demographics of your club. Most clubs try and staff their businesses with people who are too young, thinking that they are saving money.

In most markets, paying about two dollars more than the local minimum wage will get you talent, as opposed to just warm bodies filling job slots. Local minimum wage is what you would have to pay to get someone to take a front counter job. In northern states, it might be as much as $12 to 15 per hour. In the southern states, it could be much less.

Add two dollars to that amount and you can usually upgrade your quality of hire. Two dollars an hour is about $360 a month, or about half of one membership. Talent will lead to production, which is what you what to hire for your new business.

Also consider having fewer part-timers and more long-term employees who you have invested in through education and staff development. A hardworking former housewife returning to the work force who has had work experience in the past can often do more work in 40 hours than part-time people can do in 60 hours.

Payroll, payroll taxes, bonuses, and commissions should be between 37 and 42 percent of the entire monthly operating expense. Do not base your payroll on total sales for the club (total revenue). The fitness business is a fixed-cost business, meaning that at some point, once you hit a certain level, everything after that point should become profit. Payrolls that are too big eat up the profitability of most new clubs. Run lean through your first six months and only add staff as needed.

To be successful in the future, you have to move toward an older, more mature, and more productive staff that matches the demographics of your club.

The best staff is working and won't usually answer want ads. Look for people with business sense and not necessarily people who have prior fitness-business experience. You can teach fitness, but business sense is harder to teach. Managers at Gap® stores, people working in GNC® stores, and other folks who are working in customer service-centered jobs make great employees because they are have had good training but are usually looking for jobs with better pay and more enjoyable atmospheres, such as fitness businesses.

IHRSA can also provide an invaluable resource for staffing through its jobsite, www.activecareers.com, and you can also meet a number of fitness professionals looking for work due to transfers and moves, or just out of school, by attending IHRSA tradeshows and other regional IHRSA events.

The Key Concept in This Chapter

Staffing will be your biggest challenge in your business. Finding the right staff and motivating each person to produce is an important thing to learn early in your career. Attend all the seminars you can, especially major IHRSA events that feature a variety of speakers who address the unique concerns of staffing in this industry.

Additional Resources

IHRSA's Active Careers website, the premier resource for fitness industry professionals, connects industry-specific job seekers with job openings at fitness clubs and companies located around the world. ActiveCareers contains job postings, HR news, health club employee testimonials, compensation data, information about various industry positions including job descriptions, and much more! www.activecareers.com

Sample job descriptions: http://www.activecareers.com/employer

IHRSA Tip—Job Descriptions: Why and How to Use Them

Generally, U.S. federal law does not require written job descriptions. However, these documents can be useful to employers, employees, and job applicants with respect to:

- Recruiting, interviewing, and selecting employees
- Training and orienting new employees
- Establishing performance requirements
- Evaluating the performance of employees
- Making decisions about compensation and/or job restructuring
- Checking for compliance with legal requirements related to equal opportunity, equal pay, overtime eligibility, etc.
- Providing proof of the essential functions of a job, for purposes of the Americans with Disabilities Act (ADA)
- Providing evidence that practices are fair, should an owner need to defend them in court

Components of effective job descriptions

- Job descriptions document an employee's major functions or duties, responsibilities, and/or other critical features, such as skill, effort, and working conditions. Key components include:
- Title of the position
- Department
- Reports to (to whom the person directly reports)
- Overall responsibility
- Key areas of responsibility, with approximate percentage of time spent on each area (using action verbs when possible)
- Consults with (those people with whom the person works on a regular basis)
- Terms of employment (full-time, part-time, seasonal, etc.)
- Qualifications (educational, work experience, etc.)
- Disclaimers (to remind readers that the job description is not meant to be all-inclusive, that the job itself is subject to change, and that the document

does not constitute an employment contract.) For example: "Nothing in this job description restricts management's right to assign or reassign duties and responsibilities to this job at any time. This job description does not constitute a written or implied contract of employment."

Essential functions

Language in job descriptions should effectively establish the nature and importance of essential functions without being prejudicial to individuals with disabilities. Focus on essential functions in terms of what they actually require, not simply the ways in which they have customarily been performed. Give some notion of frequency, intensity, and/or duration (to help establish the level of the work demand). For example, the word "typically" can be used to acknowledge the possibility that alternate manners of performance of a function may be reasonable, as determined on a case-by-case basis.

For example, the essential functions may be written as follows:

- Frequently lifts, carries, or otherwise moves and positions objects weighing up to 50 pounds when stocking the supply room and setting up equipment
- Typically bends, stoops, and crouches on a regular basis to adjust settings on equipment

Clauses such as "performs other duties as assigned" are generally not suitable for covering essential functions. If a task is essential, it should be described.

Avoiding legal pitfalls

Job descriptions are generally regarded as legal documents. They have the potential to become the subject of contention, including grievances or litigation. It is critical that accuracy be maintained. Designate one party (for example, the supervisor or human resources director) as having primary responsibility for keeping job descriptions current, and have a plan for reviewing them on a regular basis.

Avoid any references in job descriptions to race, color, religion, age, sex, national origin or nationality, or physical or mental disability. Finally, to avoid claims of age discrimination, experience should not include an upper limit.

Visit www.activecareers.com to download samples of fitness industry job descriptions.

Note: This tip is intended to provide general information, and does not constitute legal advice.

10

Sales and Marketing Are Part of All Small Businesses

If owning a fitness business was only as simple as it sounds. You run a little marketing, sign up the hundreds of folks driven crazy by your latest ad, and then spend the rest of the day counting money and working out. If this scenario were true, a lot more clubs would be open around the country, because everyone would want to be in the business.

Marketing and sales are fundamental skills that every new owner will need to be successful over time, especially since you cannot separate the two in a small business. Marketing can be simply defined as getting qualified butts in seats. While this task sounds simple enough for an owner to accomplish, the job of actually getting qualified leads in the door of your new business takes two distinct skills that you must master to be successful.

First, you have to have a marketing plan in place that will attract new prospective members to the gym. Secondly, once the prospective member is in the facility, you have to have a trained salesperson in place to take advantage of the marketing dollars you spent to drive that person through the door.

Marketing and sales are totally dependent on each other in your club's business plan. Unlike other areas of the club, such as personal training and group exercise, where you can excel in one and be terrible in the other and still run a successful business, you cannot be strong in marketing or sales and weak in the other and survive over time. You have to master both to be successful and these two areas, along with staffing, may be the most difficult areas of the fitness business.

You can make a number of classic mistakes as a new, or even seasoned, owner. One of the most harmful situations over time is an owner who never realizes that everything he presents to the public becomes part of his brand in the market. An owner on the wrong track will run ads with a very short-term vision. This type of ad is put together at the very last minute, has the standard components of a semi-naked model, a list of all the stuff in the club, and a price special.

Over time, your club becomes know for these poorly presented ads that aren't consistent and don't build a positive brand over time, thereby often lowering the perceived value of your business. Marketing should be viewed as a long-term endeavor that gets better results over time and eventually leads to a strong and consistent identity in the marketplace.

You only really have two options for your new business when it comes to attracting new members. You can run price ads, which are based upon offering a sale or discount of some type, or exposure ads, which means that you use marketing to introduce your business to new people without them having to take on any risk or part with any money before getting a chance to try it.

Note: Some of the material in this chapter is excerpted from *Anyone Can Sell*, by Thomas Plummer (Healthy Learning, 2007).

Marketing Basics

In the ancient days of the fitness industry, which means prior to 1990, marketing was somewhat simple. You ran an ad with a price special of some type and people showed up. You could also use draw boxes (enter here to win 50 gallons of gas, etc.) and people not only picked up the phone but also actually came in and joined. Even better were referrals from members, who gladly gave out lists of their friends who needed to join the gym and who really did respond to the club's calls.

All of these things that worked then are no longer effective, because the market is different. This difference can be simply explained by the following formula:

<u>High demand</u> = Almost any marketing will work
Limited choices

Simply put, this equation means that if you own the only bar in a college town, you'll make a ton of money. In other words, if you have high demand (thousands of thirsty college students) coupled with limited choices (you own the only bar), you will make a fortune, no matter what specials you run or advertising you do, if indeed you have to do any at all.

This equation held up in the early days of the fitness industry. More people wanted to join gyms than there were choices. Therefore, any fitness ad worked and you looked like a genius no matter what you ran.

The issue is that no one ever realized that it wasn't the ads the drove the business; it was the market at the time. Ads in those days were price driven, which means that you ran some type of special that deviated from your normal pricing structure. For example, your club might have a regular membership fee of $69, but in your ad in the paper you feature a two-for-one summer special where two people can join for the price of just one membership.

This ad might work for a month or two and then the club owner would switch to another special, such as join now (during the summer) and get the fall for free. The member would join in the summer and defer the first payment until after the first of the year. This process would go on month after month as the owner grinded out deal after deal after deal. "Hey, what special are you guys running this week?" was a common customer question in those days.

Everything you did in those days worked, so it had to be the marketing right? Wrong. Price-driven marketing, as illustrated in the earlier formula, will work as long as the demand stays higher than the choices available. Another way to look at it is as follows: If you own something that is limited or rare, you can charge a lot more for it than you could if it was more common. If you have a high demand for fitness, which the industry did in the 1980s, and limited fitness choices compared to what the consumer currently has, then almost any ad or special you might run would work.

Things changed in the 1990s and into the early 2000s. Demand stayed flat compared to the percentage of total population, but the number of clubs began increasing. The market was still somewhat strong, but it was becoming harder to do the old-style marketing and still drive big numbers. Other factors, such as increasingly sophisticated consumers, also started to change the way marketing worked. The new formula for those years looked as follows:

$$\frac{\textbf{Flat demand and growth}}{\textbf{Increasing consumer options}} = \frac{\textbf{Decline in the effectiveness}}{\textbf{of traditional marketing}}$$

Pressure selling has always been a part of the industry, but it became worse when the marketing became less effective. If you have fewer people responding to your ads, then the pressure has to shift to the salespeople. The chains in the late 1980s and 1990s were notorious for the pressure their salespeople had to apply at the point of sale, as well as the stress felt by those sales teams to make their 100 cold calls a day and keep their personal appointment sheets filled. When the marketing began to fail, the pressure was on for the salespeople to fill the shortages. The current market follows yet another formula:

$$\frac{\textbf{Slightly increasing demand}}{\textbf{Virtually unlimited fitness choices}} = \frac{\textbf{Failure of traditional price}}{\textbf{ads to drive revenue}}$$

This equation shows where the market is in 2006/2007 and will be for a number of years to come. When you have an increasing demand for fitness by the consumer, yet not enough demand to keep up with the increase in club openings, price-driven marketing works even less effectively than in the earlier models.

Price-driven ads are by design meant to generate volume. You can't sell your product at the regular price so you discount it and hope to sell more to make up the difference. In other words, if your price is $40 for an item and it doesn't sell, then can you discount it with hopes to sell a higher number to make up for lesser money earned through the lower price?

Two key elements are in play that also lead to the failure of price-driven advertising in this model. Only a finite number of people are joining a club at any given time. At this point in time, only about 16 percent of the population in this country belongs to a health club or fitness facility of any type, and even though this number might be increasing, it is not rising as quickly as new clubs are opening.

As an owner, you are locked into competing for a finite number of members that might join. If you are using price alone to attract new members, which again is a system designed to generate a high volume of new memberships, your business plan fails because an insufficient number of new people are interested in joining a fitness facility in the first place. In other words, you are running ads to attract people who aren't there.

The second reason you would be on the track to failure is that price ads work off a false assumption. This assumption states that price ads are created to attract people who *already have* fitness experience and are not designed to attract new people who have never been in a fitness facility in the past.

For example, a typical price ad might look as follows:

Join now and get the rest of the summer free!
- **Large free-weight area**
- **100 group classes a week**
- **Free childcare**
- **Certified personal trainers**
- **Weight loss available**
- **Tanning included with every membership**

Couple this copy with a picture of a semi-naked woman and you have the typical fitness ad you would see in a shopper, newspaper, or Yellow Pages ad. Besides being somewhat illogical in the sense that a fitness center is advertising that it has fitness stuff in it, this ad is also ineffective because it targets the wrong market. Think of a hotel advertising that it has beds or a car dealership advertising that it has cars for sale. "Hey, come to our fitness center, we have fitness stuff."

Think about this sample ad carefully. All of these bullet points are aimed at whom? Would a deconditioned female respond to this ad? Or is the more likely respondent a person who already has fitness experience and is looking for these things in a gym?

Also think about the statistic that only about 16 percent of the population belongs to a fitness facility at this point in time. If all clubs run these types of ads, which again most do, then all fitness owners do is target that same small population. This advertising is doing nothing to attract people who don't have any experience and who don't respond to these ads.

Exposure Marketing

If you don't advertise price, then all you have left is exposure marketing. Remember that only two ways exist to attract people to a fitness business. You either offer a price special of some type or let you let the person come and try your facility, see if he likes it, and then sign him up.

Some non-ads run pretty pictures and let people know the business exists without any offering type of special. Coke™ and its traditional bear ads during the holidays are a great example. These ads are cute, but they don't offer any special offer. You watch, smile, and maybe connect with the company somehow.

You aren't Coke and you don't have the money to run ads that merely look cute. In this business, you have to run ads that drive people to the door in big enough numbers to feed your business, so every ad has to have some device to elicit a response.

Exposure marketing means that you let someone come try your business for free and see if the person likes it enough to join. This type of marketing is called trial marketing, and it is a very common form of advertising.

Full trial memberships, meaning those trials that last seven days or longer as opposed to just a single workout, have been used in the fitness business since about 1990 and are an effective way to attract people who normally wouldn't respond to any type of traditional fitness advertising. A sample trial ad might look as follows:

Never been in a fitness club before?
Afraid to take that first step?

**Would you like to try the area's only upscale fitness center
for 14 days with no risk or obligation?**

**We are so proud of our club that we would like you to come try us
absolutely free for 14 days with no risk to you or any obligation.
We're proud of our club and feel it is the best in town, but talk is
cheap. We would like you to come meet our staff and meet the
other members and try a full membership for a full 14 days.**

**At the end of this trial, if we haven't earned your business,
then we don't deserve to have you as a member.**

**All trial memberships include a personal coach, a session with a
nutrition professional, and a full membership to the club for 14 days**

This type of copy is aimed at the people in your market who aren't fitness people and who again don't respond to typical price-driven ads. The thing to remember is that people with fitness experience will find you anyway, since fitness is part of their lives. Those folks are looking for a gym as soon as they move to a new area or get bored with their existing facility.

Exposure ads also kill risk, which through the years has proven to be the biggest barrier to inquiry for those who don't have any fitness experience. Risk pops up in the form of, "What if I try this and don't like it? Will I still have to pay for it? Why can't I try it first and see if I like it?"

All of these concerns and questions are legitimate and don't get answered through traditional price-driven ads. Traditional ads, coupled with traditional sales techniques that slam hard on the first day a new person inquires about the club, set up an almost impenetrable wall for someone without fitness experience who might be nervous about inquiring at a fitness center for the first time.

The Trial Philosophy

The trial philosophy is really nothing more than stating that you have a good club and you'd like people to come try it because you know that once they do they'll want to become a member. The trial philosophy can be explained as it was in the previous ad copy:

Would you like to try our club absolutely free for a full 14 days, with no risk, no obligation, and no money up front? We'd like you to come try our club, meet our members, and meet our staff. At the end of 14 days, if we haven't earned your business, then we don't deserve to have you as a member.

This type of marketing not only generates a larger number of leads, but also makes the salesperson's job a lot easier too. Trials are targeted at people who don't have a lot of fitness experience, which is a much larger number than those who do. Trials done correctly feed the club sufficient leads, which allows the salespeople to concentrate on closing the ones already in the system rather than wasting time trying to develop appointments that never show.

Types of trials

A club owner could use two types of trials. A regular trial simply lets anyone in the market who is qualified try the club for the set trial period.

Qualification is usually determined through the following restrictions:

- Must be 18 or older (minimum age may depend upon the type of club)
- Must live in the club's market area (as shown with a driver's license or equivalent ID)
- Must show ability to buy at some point by flashing a credit card
- May be used once a year

These points represent the fine print. You will still have a small percentage, usually about 3 to 4 percent of all the people who take the trial, who don't really have any intention of actually becoming a member. This situation is acceptable for two reasons. First, the person might actually buy something while in the club, such as a bottle of water or personal training, so the risk is acceptable for these people. The cost of actually servicing these members is low compared to the upside of what they might spend in the club during the trial visits. It is also important to remember that just because a person doesn't join during this trial period doesn't mean he might not consider joining in the future based upon his experience with your club.

Second, this number represents a very small percentage to worry about if indeed the volume of potential members walking through the door does increase. In other words, if the volume goes up for potential members, it doesn't really matter if a few of them are just passing through looking for a free workout or two. The key is to avoid losing focus on what you're trying to accomplish with a trial. The goal is to drive more guests, from a different group, than you would get with regular advertising.

The trial philosophy is really nothing more than stating that you have a good club and you'd like people to come try it because you know that once they do they'll want to become a member.

Length of trials in use

A number of variations can be used with trial memberships. The examples listed in this section are the most commonly used in today's market.

The seven-day trial. This trial length is used by clubs that just opened or with a customer who has never used the trial before and is a little nervous. The guest has total use of the club for seven consecutive days.

The 14-day trial. This trial length is the standard for most clubs. It's long enough to attract more people than the seven-day trial, but the right length for most clubs to service without losing control.

The 21-day trial. This trial length is a specialty trial a club owner would use in conjunction with the 14-day offer. The 21-day trial would be offered to small businesses or as a special pass. For example, a sales manager might visit a small business and offer the owner and her eight employees a chance to come try the gym as a group. Rather than handing out almost worthless business-card size passes, and to show more value than the 14-day trial available in the paper, the salesperson would hand the owner eight 21-day trials in the form of 4 x 5 cards with an employee's name handwritten on each.

Paid trials. Paid trials are a form of target-specific marketing, which means that you are using a specially designed tool to go after very small segments of the market. Another way to think about it is to imagine a single bullet rather than a shotgun approach. Traditional marketing done through newspaper ads, for example, works off the principle of sending a mass message to the entire market with hopes that someone reading the paper will see your message. Target-specific marketing, on the other hand, assumes that you can identify one specific person, or group of people, who is an ideal candidate for your club and then you offer that person or group a specifically designed marketing piece targeting their needs and concerns.

Sample paid trials, such as six weeks for $69, also represent a finite course of action. One of the problems with traditional fitness membership offerings is that they don't match what the consumer is actually looking for when he walks through the door. For example, a deconditioned female walks through the door with the specific concern of losing 10 pounds before being in her sister's wedding in a few months. She has a specific need, a specific goal, and a set timeline in mind when she comes through the door.

The sale breaks down when 30 minutes later a salesperson hammers her on a long-term commitment, or even a simple month-to-month membership, both of which fail to meet the goal she had when she came through the door. She wants to buy a specific solution for a specific problem, which is what you should be selling her. Solve her problem first and she is more likely to stay beyond the initial program. The trial membership, again a short-term course for a flat fee, gives her what she wants and also helps the club in that it exposes its services and programs to someone who might not sign up through standard fitness offerings.

Paid trials can be used throughout the year and work especially well in softer delivery systems that cater to women, such as Val-Paks® and other coupon- or value-driven tools. Sample paid-trial copy might read as follows:

We know the first 10 pounds are always the hardest... and we also know that you may not know how to get started.

Our "six weeks for $69" easy-start program includes everything you need to lose that first 10, including a personal coach who will guide you every step of the way.

Need to lose weight for that special event?
Interested in fitness but don't know where to start?
Overwhelmed by too much information about fitness?

Our six-week program is the perfect way to get started on the right path to fitness and weight management with no risk or any further obligation.

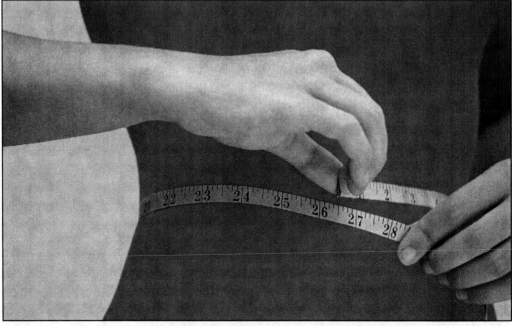

Paid trials can be used throughout the year and work especially well in softer delivery systems that cater to women

The Law of Diminishing Returns

Price-driven ads do work for a short period of time in most markets, but ultimately fail in almost every market. This failure happens because of the law of diminishing returns.

This theory, derived from an agriculture concept born in Europe, states that when you first plant a crop in a new field your harvest from that same crop in that same field will go down in each succeeding year. For example, you might plant corn and generate 20 bushels per acre the first year. If you plant corn again in the same field next year, your harvest will drop to maybe 18 bushels per acre and continue to drop each year after that until your harvest reaches a sustainable low point.

In other words, by repeating the same action over and over again you get lower and lower responses. Over time, you will ultimately hit a low point where the action generates the lowest possible number for that field or market. In the corn example, you might get to the point where you are down to a few bushels per acre, at which point it bottoms out.

Price-driven ads emulate this same theory in the fitness business. Run the same type of ad over and over again and slowly that market is burned up and the ad fails. For example, when an owner first runs price-driven ads, he will get results, but if he continues to run them, the market becomes burned over time and the ad response continues to drop until it hits the lowest sustainable number.

For example, if an owner offers a year's membership at $489 in the paper, he will initially be successful by attracting everyone in the market looking for a membership who is willing to pay $489. After the owner burns up that segment, however, then what are his options? If everyone in his market who wants to, or can, pay $489 has responded, then each time he runs that ad it will be less successful as fewer people are left to respond.

This owner's next step would be to lower his price, perhaps to $449. He would thereby open up his market to a new segment that didn't respond to his previous ads at $489 per year and he might generate a little success with this ad for a short period of time.

But what happens when new sales falter again? When an owner is dependent on price-driven ads he will ultimately burn up his market, which is nothing more than the law of diminishing returns kicking in, and eventually he will be forced to lower his price to the lowest common denominator, which might be $249 or even less in this example.

Every market will have a limit, no matter what the price.

Can you use a low price based upon a monthly membership that resists the theory of diminishing returns? What happens, for example, if you run prices so low that everyone in the market who has ever thought about a fitness membership has no excuse left? The ads will still fail over time, but it will take longer for it to happen.

For example, an owner runs prices in the $9-per-month range. This price will obviously attract the widest number of potential members who are interested in price and the theory is that this price is so low that he should be able to attract new members practically forever. This type of pricing is the purest form of a volume-driven business plan because almost all his revenue is coming from building up a large membership check based upon thousands of people paying him $9 per month.

The reality is that every market still has a limit. If you use the low price of $9, then you might be targeting a huge number in your market. This number is called penetration rate and is the total percentage of the population you can attract to your business.

Penetration rate has two limiting factors: drive time from your business and turnover in your market. Research shows that the average person will only drive about 12 minutes from their home to get to a fitness facility. Typical facilities, for example, usually have about 85 to 90 percent of their membership living within a 12-minute drive time from their club. Specialty clubs, such as women-only or lifestyle-enhancing centers (personal training) draw from a slightly larger area, with a drive-time potential of up to 20 minutes.

In other words, every club has a geographical range that limits its drawing power to an equivalent of about three to five miles from the club. Potential members simply won't drive any further than that to go to a club for a workout.

The turnover in an area also is a factor. Some markets, such as parts of Orlando or Atlanta, have extremely high turnover in their younger segments. These areas have a larger than normal amount of apartments and other multifamily homes, which turn over often due to the large number of young workers coming into and out of the area. This number is usually constant, however, and once accounted for becomes a normal part of the business plan.

For example, the owner using the $9-per-month per-member price is targeting 20 percent of his available market. If his five-mile market ring contains 60,000 people, then his business plan is based upon attracting about 12,000 members paying $9 per month. He would hit this number near the end of the second year if his business plan came together, meaning his monthly check before collection expenses and losses would be approximately $108,000. It is possible for the owner to get to this point and several low-cost chains have clubs that do these numbers. The hardest part is sustaining these numbers over time.

Once this owner hits a certain penetration rate, then that point is as far as he can go with this type of business plan. Everyone who wants a membership at $9 has already joined and, over time, the owner will reap lower and lower responses from the same type of advertising.

Also remember that his market has geographical limits that prevent him from pulling more members from further away from the club. If his club has unusual turnover numbers, he might be able to sustain higher volume over time, but eventually that number will also top out because of the loss rate.

Price Ads Versus Trials Memberships

What everyone who uses price ads forgets is that price ads are designed to attract people who have previous experience with fitness and do nothing to develop new business. If you know about fitness and are looking for a place to workout, then price ads will work. Price ads won't work, however, for people who don't have this experience and aren't sure whether fitness is really for them or not.

Trial ads, on the other hand, are based upon an entirely different theory. Trial memberships, and the variety of copy that supports these ads, are designed to develop interest in people who have not yet taken the next step toward fitness. The most important thing to remember is that price ads fail over time and trial memberships don't, because the former are designed to capture people already interested in fitness and the latter are designed to develop new markets over time.

In summary, trial memberships done correctly help drive new sales because over time these ads will continue to increase the number of potential members who visit a gym. Trial ads also don't weaken over time because repeated use doesn't burn the market as price-driven ads do. The major weakness of price-driven ads is that eventually the responsibility to fill the club with potential members will fall upon the sales team, because the ads will fail to drive enough new bodies over time.

Sales teams in clubs using trial memberships should concentrate on getting these trial members into the club and then spend a great deal of their time and energy servicing these potential members. Keep in mind that trial members will usually revisit the club more than once, and clubs using trials will always have a combination of new business and recurring leads running through the business each day. The recurring aspect of a trial system eliminates the dependency on having to fill the club's appointment book each day with fresh leads that then have to be pressured into closing during their first visit or lost forever because you only had one shot at getting the sale.

The Marketing Budget

You should budget about 10 percent of your base operating expense each month for outside marketing to attract new leads to your business. The national average, according to research, is that the average club that is struggling only spends about 4 percent of its budget each month on marketing, while more financially successful clubs will spend about 10 percent.

What should you spend this budget on each month?

You will be better off doing fewer things, but mastering these things in your market. Many owners take the shotgun approach and spend a little money on a lot of things over a year's time. Unfortunately, the combination of these things, because they all look a little different and are done by different ad people, doesn't lead to brand recognition and more sales in the market.

Consider track marketing when you first get started. Track marketing means that you start with an ad concept and then stay with that theme and colors over time. For example, maybe the best-known track marketing ads are the ones starring the Pillsbury® Doughboy™. That company has run the Doughboy ads for about 40 years and it's hard for the average consumer to hear the word "Pillsbury" and not add "Doughboy" to the end.

The track concept means that Pillsbury changes their ads often, but has the same components in each ad. You always see the happy family, a warm kitchen, and the Doughboy somewhere in the ad. Each ad is different, but in reality each ad is always the same. This approach builds brand recognition over time. People are more likely to buy something from a company that has been around for a while and that they are familiar with.

You can use the following tools to develop track marketing. The *IHRSA Resource Guide* has a list of the better-known marketing companies in the business. As you shop these companies, look for total support and guidance and don't always go for the cheapest price. Marketing builds your brand and you want to work with a company that can take you as far as you want to go.

Direct mail cards. These cards are sent directly to the consumer each month from the marketing company you choose. You can control where the cards are sent through the use of a carrier route radius report, which is usually free from the company you are working with for your marketing.

Carrier route radius reports list every mailing address in a radius from the club based upon mileage. You can also narrow your mailings down by household income. See Chapter 4 for more information on carrier route radius reports.

Several tricks can make your direct mail cards more successful. Only use the oversized cards. They cost a few cents more, but these cards are long enough to stick out from the rest of the mail and getting seen is the biggest part of getting results.

You should also drop your cards in the mail every Monday. Some companies want you to drop the entire month's mailing all at once, but the risk of not getting seen is higher when using that technique. For example, suppose you drop 20,000 cards during the first week, but you catch a heavy direct mail day where Sears®, Radio Shack®, and Home Depot® are all dropping their pieces as well. You will be lost in the bulk and your ads for the month will be less effective.

Drop weekly and you are bound to get through, in addition to developing a steady stream of guests throughout the month. Direct mail does not work in every market, but you should at least give your campaign six months to determine if it indeed works for you. Shop for prices. The cost will vary depending on how many cards you send each month and how long you commit to mailing each month.

Flyer inserts. Flyer inserts are the cheapest marketing you can do and are also good for presales. This tool is 8½ x 11 inches, one-sided, full-color, and is stuffed in the newspaper. The cost varies by newspaper, but you can control where your pieces go by zone or zip code, depending on which the paper chooses to use.

The best days to insert are Mondays, Tuesdays, and Thursdays, if possible. Avoid Wednesdays if you can because that is traditionally food day in most papers, meaning

You should budget about 10 percent of your base operating expense each month for outside marketing to attract new leads to your business.

that they are stuffed with flyers from all the local grocery stores. Prices depend on the newspaper and the quality of the piece. If the paper lets you use the back, fill it up but don't pay double for it.

Internal marketing. This tool is often an overlooked part of the marketing plan. Each month, you should send a quality letter to all of your members, driving referrals through promotions, such as inviting them to bring a guest this month and choose from the following three things: three months added to your membership, a $150 personal-training package, or a $100 shopping spree in the club. Start this program the first month you are open and do it every month after that point. These letters, which your marketing company should help you generate, usually cost approximately $0.70 to $0.90 each.

Cable and radio ads. The cost of these ads depends upon the market. Radio is usually too expensive, but it might be worth trying in smaller markets where the station choice is more limited and the ads are less expensive. Radio also might be part of your presale approach, since you are trying to flood the market during the first months you are open.

Cable ads are very much dependent on the local television stations and whether you have more than one club or not. If you would like to try these ads, the best time of the year is late September through early November. Don't spend extra money for direct placement in your favorite television show. To get the most bang for your buck, ask for rotational advertising, where your ads might pop up any time during the day or night. You'll get more ads this way and a higher chance of being seen by a wider range of people. You will save money as well.

Newspaper ads. Large newspaper ads are a good tool for presales, especially if you have the budget to go big. Newspapers do not work in every market and are definitely a try-and-see venue. Most newspapers have a very large percentage of ads as compared to stories and pictures and it is very hard to get noticed in large, metro newspapers. Smaller markets, however, still have some life and you can usually buy bigger ads for a reduced cost. If you commit to an annual contract in the smaller-market papers, you can often get a full-page ad once a month for less than $2,000 per insert. If the market is right, the ad combined with inserts is a strong tool.

Web pages. Web pages are at best "B" level marketing, which means that you have to have one, but you don't want to overdo it and spend stupid money. A functional web page should cost less than $1,000 to set up and cost less than $200 per month to maintain. For this money, you should get a site that changes copy every day, has a capture tool (e.g., to get this free trial, submit your email address now) that helps you get leads, and gives you the ability to post your own schedules and events. Make sure you own your own domain name and that you have clear documentation of where your site is being housed/served. If the company that does your page goes out of business, you want the ability to get your name and site moved to another server.

Learning to Sell Is the First Step to Success

You sell. It's what you do every day in the fitness business. It's been an inherent part of the business since it began and it will always be a vital part of what you do for a living. In fact, 95 percent of what you do in this business, and virtually any other small business, is sell somebody something every day. Sales are how you make money and how you keep cash flow, the lifeblood of small business, flowing through your ever-needy businesses every day, every week, and every month you are operating.

Once you make this money from sales you can then spend the other 5 percent of your time sitting up in your bed at 3:00 in the morning counting your money and trying to figure out just what happened in your business that day. Owners usually make most of their money in the fitness business on the floor or behind that front counter, helping people get what they want and solving the problems they bring as part of their expectations of membership.

Most new owners drift away from this core philosophy at some point early in their careers. They start on the floor with the members, but it's just a matter of time before they move to the office. They sit and look at statements, make deposits, return phone calls, solve member service issues, make up their own ads, call the significant other, sneak a lunch, fix a toilet, run a few errands, and, at the end of the day, they're sitting on the couch feeling really tired from putting in a full day at the gym.

The problem is that they forgot to make any money that day because they were too busy being busy. They started as production-based people, but they eventually become managers, and managers seldom make the money. This does not mean that you have to be selling memberships in your own business forever. It does mean that you often lose this production mentality by moving off the floor and into the office setting.

Any time you find a business that isn't performing, one of the first questions that has to be asked of the owner is, "How many memberships did you sell in your own business last month?" If the business is flat, the answer is usually zero. This owner, who probably started as a driven salesperson putting memberships down every night and growing the receivable base and cash flow, probably comes in at 10:00 in the morning, takes care of paperwork, checks the deposits, and is gone by 6:00 at the latest.

When times get tough, most owners just get more entrenched in their offices. "If I just sit here long enough and refigure these numbers, sooner or later they'll get better." The recommendation is get off your butt and go back to work, because one of the fundamental principles in this business is that no one ever made any money in the fitness business sitting at a computer in an office.

Even the owners who are running successful businesses and are far removed from sales need to sell a few memberships in their businesses each month just to keep the feel. You can ask your staff a lot of questions about what's going on with the potential members, but when you do a sale yourself you get instant feedback from the person's words and expressions, which gives you the powerful information you need to keep that business successful.

In the fitness business, you make your money on the floor, one membership at a time. You also make it selling training sessions, soft drinks, supplements, tanning, and any other profit centers the club offers. The old staff training line, "Can I get you a drink for the ride home?" is often more powerful than a whole lot of hours spent sitting at that desk wondering how much money the club will save switching from three-ply toilet paper to the cheap stuff. Small business owners must remember the following principle:

You can never save yourself into profitability.

Most fitness businesses can be cut back and waste exists in every small business. In fact, it is hard to find any fitness business that cannot trim 10 percent or so from its base operating cost.

The secret to running a successful fitness business, however, is not saving pennies. It's making dollars. You are in a production-based business, which means that every day the club is open someone has to sell someone else something. Again, 95 percent of what you do in the fitness business is produce. It takes work to keep this production happening in most small businesses, especially if you get into multiple units or get big enough where you actually do work as a manager in your own business.

One of the main obstacles to keeping this production-based environment going is that managers and owners often take too much on that gets in the way of making money. The basic rule of thumb is that if it gets in the way of production, farm it out. Think of keeping your business a lean, mean selling machine. If something gets in the way of that mentality, you probably shouldn't be doing it.

For example, many young owners, and even a few experienced ones, insist on collecting their own memberships. Why would you not farm this task out to a specialist and then manage the results instead of doing the work yourself? In many cases, owners simply can't help doing this work, since this industry attracts so many control freaks whose idea of running a business is, "Get the hell out of my way and I'll do this myself." The sad thing is that when this owner says, "I'll do this" it usually means everything in the business except the important things, such as selling memberships, training, and other high-dollar items that would give the club a cash flow boost that day.

The goal is to keep the business simple. Farm out everything that gets in the way of production and keep the business totally focused on putting numbers up on the board every day. In the fitness industry, you make your money one day at a time, and your focus should be to keep the business on a set production track each day.

Another mistake that owners make in their quest for building a superior production-based business is that they forget *when* they make the money. Most clubs have a prime time, and that key production slot is seldom between noon and 5:00 in the afternoon. In other words, most owners go home just when the business is starting to get good.

Numbers-wise, owners make about 70 percent of their money in a coed club between roughly 4:00 and 9:00 in the evening Monday through Thursday and on Saturday morning from about 8:00 to 1:00. If you have a women-only club, you usually have a second prime time in the morning during the week, from about 8:00 to 11:00.

If you are going to score each day, then you have to have your best players, without exception, in the club during these prime hours. If you leave at 5:00 and let your less-capable brother-in-law run your business for the rest of the evening, you will eventually fail, simply because no strong players are present to drive the business.

It's hard to make money when you're not in the business during those best production hours. Even if you've matured, you still have to have a powerful driver in the business during these times. If you are an owner with a single business, then it is absolutely mandatory that you are in your business for those key hours during which you will make money in this business.

When you explore ways to improve your business, always return to the key questions: "Am I doing everything possible to create a business that is totally production-based?" Another way to look at this question is to ask yourself: "Is what I am doing, or going to do, the best use of my time and my manager's time at this minute?" If what you're doing is not driving production and sales, then you should be doing something else. As you increase your knowledge about sales, always return to the most basic but powerful premise in the fitness business:

95 percent of what you do in this business is sell somebody something every day.

Have this statement made into a huge sign that hangs over your desk. Also make this rule one of the first things all new employees learn, along with your new definition of sales, on their first day on the job.

If you want to be successful in this business, learn to sell and get some practical sales experience before you open your club. Do not assume that you can just hire a bunch of people to sell memberships for you. A good sales effort takes training and leadership every single day, as well an immense amount of follow-up.

If you can't sell memberships in your own club, it is unlikely that you can teach someone else to do it and manage the results. This statement is especially true of those trainers who want to open their own training facilities. Opening your own business doesn't mean that you simply get to train more people in a bigger room.

When you open this new business, you should be moving from the training floor to the sales and management floor, and the only training you should be doing is training other trainers to be successful and training the rest of your staff in what takes to be a financially solid production-based business.

How good do you have to be?

You need to be able to close at least 55 percent of all your qualified guests with an annual membership over a 30-day period of time. This number assumes that you are using some type of trial membership and that some of your members will need more than one workout before they can buy. In other words, you should end up with 55 new members on annual memberships out of every 100 qualified guests who walk through the door.

Out of these 55 people, at least 30 percent should buy during their first visit. These sales come in form of buddy sales, referrals, or just folks who come into the club ready to buy. Remember, these sales are annual memberships, not a bunch of short-term or daily members. Your goal is to create a large receivable base, and adding annual members each month is how it is done.

The national average is that the typical club only closes approximately 38 percent of all its qualified traffic over a 30-day period. This low number is due to lack of training, poor systems, and the absence of a set follow-up that goes beyond just calling and harassing people on the phone. If you are using a different system, such as more open-ended memberships, adjust accordingly, but you still have to establish a standard that will help you get the most members possible from your leads.

You will be more effective if you learn to enhance rather than discount. Enhancing the sale means that you recognize that the person is graciously giving you his business and that you reward that choice by giving him a gym bag, T-shirt, a personal-training package, and a few other gifts as a way of saying thanks.

The old method, which is less effective and very insulting, is to "drop close" the person by dropping $100 from the membership fee if he joins today. If the person comes back the next day, he supposedly has to pay the full price. Dropping the price the first day is meant to force the potential member to buy now rather than risk losing the $100 deal.

Everyone knows that no one ever paid the full price, and if the guest comes back the next day he can probably pay just about anything he wants to get started. Try enhancing first and offer packages to help people get started. People like to look smart, and if the customer receives a nice gift package for joining, he feels good about what he just bought.

Get control of the leads during the presale.

If you are on top of your business, then you know your leads for the day, the week, the month, the same month last year, the average per month, and maybe even the most common first name among all of your potential customers. Leads are where it all begins, and you need to get control of them from the first time the door is open for sales.

Figure 10-1 provides a sample inquiry sheet, which can be used for both walk-in traffic and phone inquiries. Do not have the guest fill this from out while he is waiting for a salesperson. The salesperson needs to be able to ask the questions as part of a normal conversation with the guest.

At the end of the day, the leads go to the sales manager, who is in charge of the club's follow-up procedures. Every phone call about membership and every guest that walks in, whether qualified or not, has to have a matching inquiry sheet on the sales manager's desk at the end of the working day.

Your third-party financial-service company should be able to provide you with sales tracking software. All leads need to be added to your ongoing file for use throughout the year, such as when sending invitations to a party or special event.

Leads are where it all begins, and you need to get control of them from the first time the door is open for sales.

Guest Profile

Today's date _____ Date recorded by manager _____

Did the person: ❏ Visit the club or ❏ Phone

Guest's or inquiry's name: _____

Have you heard about our trial membership? _____

Before we get started, may I offer you a gift from the club? _____

How did you hear about us? _____

Do you know any of our members? If so, who? _____

Have you ever been in the club before? _____

Do you work or live near the gym? _____

What type of workout are you doing now? _____

How would you classify yourself as an exerciser?

❏ I currently work out.

What are you doing? _____

How long? _____

How many days a week? _____

How is it working? _____

What are you looking for that your current program doesn't provide? _____

_____

❏ I used to work out.

What did you do at that time? _____

Were you consistent? _____

How did it work? _____

Why did you stop? _____

How are you feeling since you stopped? _____

How long have you been thinking about getting back to a regular program?_____

What's kept you from getting back in the past? _____

Is that still a problem?_____

❏ I don't work out.

What has gotten you interested in working out?_____

How do you feel about your health and condition?_____

What was the best you ever felt?_____

What was different at that time?_____

How long have you been thinking about getting into a fitness program? _____

What's kept you from getting started in the past? _____

Is that still a problem? _____

Figure 10-1. Sample inquiry sheet

We've found over the years people that who want to join a gym and begin a regular exercise program usually fall into one of three categories. Which one of these is your primary goal?

❑ Improve your appearance

❑ Improve your health

❑ Improve things in your life, such as energy level, or reduce stress

Keeping this goal in mind, what is the single most important thing you want to get out of a gym membership?_____

_____

_____

What are some other things you would like to accomplish with us?

How would you like to change your body? _____

Is your weight something you are concerned about? _____

What's the timeframe you've set for your fitness program? _____

On a scale of 1 to 10, how important is it for you to reach your personal fitness objective? _____

Is that enough to get you started and keep you coming to the gym on a regular basis? _____

Now that I have a little information about you and what you're looking for in an exercise program, may I show you the club?

Profile notes so we can best help our guest: _____

_____

Most of our guests or phone inquiries want to know more about what we do here. May we have your email address so that we can send you ongoing information about the club as well as our electronic newsletter?

Email address: _____

To thank you for taking the time to visit the club, we'd like to send you a gift. May we have your address? _____

_____

_____

What is the best phone number with which to reach you?_____

Office use only:

Club representative _____

New member _____

Trial member _____

The Key Concept in This Chapter

Marketing and sales are not separable. To be successful, you have to bring the qualified leads into the club and then give yourself the best chance possible to make each guest a new member while still maintaining proper business ethics.

New owners need to master both components in this business. They must be able to direct their marketing company regarding what they want to accomplish and be able to hire, train, and supervise an effective sales staff.

Additional Resource

IHRSA Tip—Email Marketing: Tips to make the most out of your email marketing efforts
www.ihrsa.org/tips

IHRSA Tip—Focus: The Tool for Sales Excellence
—by Karen D. Woodard

Excellence in any endeavor demands focus. Whether the area of pursuit is sports, the arts, or business, several common threads weave the fabric of success: repetition and improvement upon your best performance, desire to be the best, and a clear focus on the outcome as well as the process via which to achieve that outcome.

Achieving excellence in the craft of selling is no different. Before going further, it is important that you define excellence in selling. It is not about memorizing boilerplate techniques, nor is it about manipulation. It is about your (or your sales team's) ability to create a connection between yourself, your prospective member, and your business that results in an exchange of value for all involved parties. Thus, achieving excellence in sales is about the ability to consistently communicate in a professional, customized manner that reaches the member and moves you toward your goals.

As you read on, assess your performance, and that of your sales team. Ask yourself how often these tips are implemented—if at all. Remember, "occasionally" and "consistently" are different things with very different outcomes!

Be clear about expectations.

If you don't have the end result in mind, how can you get there? More than likely, anyone involved in sales at your club is given numbers to meet or exceed every month. That type of thing is obvious.

How clear is your sales team that their job is to create business—not simply to wait for business to come in or call? Is this job one they want to be doing and have chosen to do? Do they have clear and realistic expectations of what they will get as a result of their effort? Answering these questions will help refine everyone's clarity.

Devise a plan.

Once everyone is clear about expectations, a plan should be implemented. The simplest and most effective way to put together a plan is to use the following formula:

- Know each salesperson's goal for the period.
- Know each salesperson's closing ratio.

- Know how many tours each salesperson needs to give to reach the goal based on his closing ratio.
- Know how many appointments/tours each salesperson needs to schedule (factoring in a no-show rate of 20 to 30 percent).
- Know how many contacts each salesperson needs to schedule to reach the necessary number of appointments.

Now that the formula is outlined, a plan needs to be created to make the goals realistic and not theoretical. Once each salesperson determines the number of contacts he needs each month to reach the goal, he can determine how many leads he needs to generate to get that number of contacts (or prospects).

Each salesperson should know the average number of calls and walk-ins he personally gets each month. Those are "gimmes." For example, if Bob needs 300 leads per month and he gets 100 call-ins and walk-ins each month, then he needs to create 200 leads on his own. He will accomplish that task by consistently having a thrust in each of the following areas—the club's referral membership sales plan, its group/corporate/small business plan, its alumni member plan, its community outreach plan, and its current lead follow-up or wrap-up plan—so that he can close as much business as possible by the end of the month.

Finally, don't just create the plan and abandon it. Salespeople need to constantly monitor and make corrections so they don't find themselves coming up short of expectations at the end of the month.

Develop consistent and productive work habits.

The reality of a true professional and successful person is that they do their best and are productive all the time, not just when they feel like it or during occasional spurts of motivation. In the fitness industry, owners must be particularly diligent about this situation because the work is very social. If it's a slow sales day, the temptation is to visit and commiserate, which is even less productive. Many temptations can interfere with productivity. Ask your sales team to assess their consistency with the following activities:

- How much time do you dedicate each day to calling leads with the goal of moving the relationships forward?
- Do you enter the club every day knowing that you have a minimum of four appointments scheduled for yourself?
- Do you dedicate a minimum of two hours each week to your business development plan?

- Do you have 15 minutes, twice a day planned into your schedule for selling by wandering around?

- Do you have a wrap-up mentality, as in getting as much business in before the end of the month (or period)?

- Are you driven by (and do you practice) the belief that what you do or don't do today affects you, either positively or negatively, weeks and months down the road?

- How committed are you to a 30-minute weekly sales-skills practice session (outside of sales meetings) with a partner in your department?

Feed your belly and your brain.

Everyone knows how difficult it is to focus when your blood sugar is low from not eating enough. Sometimes you get going so fast that the day goes by without lunch, enough hydration, or even a moment to catch your breath. You know those days, when your mouth can't seem to form the sounds you need for the words you intend? Well, stop it!

Taking time out for a quick bite, a beverage, and some mental break time will do wonders for your ability to focus. Have a breakfast you enjoy, pack snacks, sip on water all day, and take an occasional break. Sales success is a conscious process, not one you can do on autopilot. With regard to feeding your belly, consider the analogy of an athlete. Do you think an endurance athlete could make it all day with no food and water?

With regard to feeding your brain, what was the last book you read or CD you listened to on your own for your own professional development? Sales success is not just about how you spend your time at work, but also about what you give focus to in your free time. If you get in the habit of reading one book per month, one publication per month, or even taking 30 minutes per week to surf the Internet for sales information, you will likely find that your focus changes dramatically—and so will your sales.

Accept no excuses from yourself.

Sometimes people say things such as, "I'm not comfortable going out and seeking referrals," "I'm tired today," or "I'm not good at asking for the sale." The reality is that you are making excuses for not being good at something. Know what your weaknesses are and change them. Do not expect them to change on their own. Ask for help. You will be amazed at what resources exist to enhance your progress.

Conclusion

How are you and your sales team doing in each of these five areas? If you make them consistent areas of focus, you can expect a higher sense of mastery, more pleasure in your work, better relationships with members and coworkers and, of course, increased sales. The choice is yours!

Karen D. Woodard is president of Premium Performance Training.

11

Presales

In the old days, presales were often months, or even years, long. In the modern market, the combination of angry attorney generals in many states, club owners who took money but never opened, and a jaded consumer who would rather just wait until the club really opens to give it money force new owners to consider other strategies.

Old presales were based upon the idea of selling memberships before the club opens and then using that money to actually build the club. If presales fall short, however, the club wouldn't open, which caused tremendous problems.

Large presales often had long-term negative consequences as well. If you sold 800 memberships in your presale, about 80 percent of those members will show up during the first two weeks you are open, leading to members who are upset because the club is too crowded and the staff doesn't know what is going on. Too many, too soon is also a problem when it comes to renewals 12 months later, when a lot of those early numbers drop away.

Soft presales are a better tool in today's market. Having a soft presale means that you only plan on preselling your club for 60 days or less and then putting most of your anticipated marketing money into the market during the first 90 days you are open. In this system, you will still get the same number of members paying dues, but you will keep more and have better word-of-mouth than you would if you were trying to make all the money before you open.

Step Presales

You can use a two- or three-step presale strategy depending on your market and the time of year you open. The best time to open is between August 15 and February 15, because that timeframe allows you to develop a strong receivable base going into the summer months of the first year you are in business.

Once you establish your opening rate, you can then start with one of the step options. For example, if you are opening on August 15, you might use a full, 60-day presale based on three steps. If your opening price was going to be $49, you would start presales in May/June at $34 and then raise it slowly, five dollars at a time, to get back to $49 when you open ($34/$39/$44 = three steps).

Two-step programs are used when your presale is shorter. It often makes sense to only presale for 30 days and get to the full price sooner. This system works better in markets where you have less competition, because you don't need to discount as much, or as early, to get memberships.

Truly upscale clubs that are basing their membership on a higher price base might only want to do a single step and presale for only 30 days. If you are basing your club on price, then no reason exists to give memberships away just to get your first generation of members.

Presale Budgets

Budget about 20 percent of your fixed expenses for each month you are preselling memberships. For example, if you expect to have a fixed budget of $70,000, and plan to resale for two months, then budget $14,000 per month for each of those months.

Once you open, budget 15 percent of your fixed expenses for the first 90 days and then move to 10 percent from that point forward. You should always be spending about 10 percent of your fixed budget each month to buy new leads and to protect your market.

Staff/Location

Most presales are done in a space adjacent to your club or in trailers (nice ones you can rent). Once you start the presale, you must have your presale location manned during the stated hours. This process can usually be handled by one or two people. Make sure your phone is answered live and that you have messaging for after-hours calls.

Create the best visuals you can about your new club. Video clips from your new group programs, actual equipment, drawings and color samples from your architect, and layouts of the club all help sell memberships.

Your Target Number

Your target number for presales is 10 percent of the members you expect to have at the end of your second year (the twenty-fifth month). If your pro formas anticipate 2,000 members at the end of the second year, then you would work toward a 200-member presale. You might do better in many markets, but this number represents the minimum you need to start your club the right way.

The First-Year Overview

Perhaps the best thing about opening your new fitness business is that you should be able to cover your monthly operating expenses between months 7 through 9 of operation. This assumption is based upon opening the club sometime in the August 15 to February 15 window.

You will also need approximately three months of reserve capital to cover your operating losses until your business plan comes together. The recommendation used to be two months of reserve, but higher rents and payroll, coupled with more competitors per market, has driven the monthly cost of operation higher and lowered the amount of new sales you can gain initially through presales.

These factors have necessitated having a higher reserve of at least three months. For example, if your anticipated cost of operation is going to be $60,000, then you need to have at least $180,000 in reserve as opposed to the $120,000 you would have needed a few years ago. Figure 11-1 illustrates a fitness business in a rental space and represents what should happen during your first year of operation from the day you formally open.

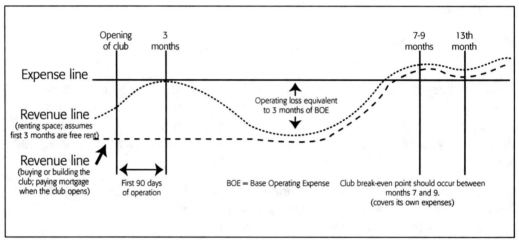

Figure 11-1. Updated maturation chart

The expense line appears somewhat constant, showing just a 5 to 10 percent increase during your first year. Most clubs are running almost at full expense when opened, because items such as the rent, bank notes, equipment leases, and utilities are already in place. The slight rise comes from adding classes or perhaps trainers as those departments grow toward their peaks.

Do not open with a full schedule of group classes. You are better off having fewer classes that are packed than having too many classes with just a few people in each. Add classes as needed, but always err toward classes being too full as opposed to too empty.

You should have revenue from day one, since you will be enrolling new members and already have the ones from your presale working out. Each guest who becomes a new member will generate revenue in the form of a membership fee and each member workout should also generate a usage fee from the club's profit centers.

The usage fee is the relationship between members who visit the club to work out (daily traffic/member check-ins) and what those same members spend in the club during each of those visits. For example, a good shake bar/coffee bar can generate $1.00 to $1.20 per member visit. This profit comes from just shakes and coffee and doesn't include cooler drinks or munchies, which have their own tracking numbers.

The good thing about profit centers is that this number should hold true even when you first open because it is based upon member visits per day and not on a total amount of members the club might have in the system. For example, if a newly opened club has 100 member check-ins for the day, it should be able to generate between $100 and 120 for the day in shakes and coffee (100 visits x $1.00 to $1.20 per visit).

Figure 11-1 shows that the expenses and revenues are close together for the first three months, and then the revenue line seems to dip. Most club owners will get the first three months free when they are in rental space, meaning that the overall expenses are lower and the revenue that is coming in will almost cover the total operating expenses.

Once the rent kicks in, however, the revenue is still below a level where it will completely cover operating expense. In Figure 11-1, the expenses don't rise, but a bigger gap appears between what is coming in and what is going out due to the rent factor.

You will also notice that this club needs three months of operating reserve (as illustrated by the dip/operating loss) before the club breaks even (incoming revenue covers total operating expense). This chart illustrates that the club covering its expenses somewhere in the seven- to nine-month period.

Revenue continues to grow and you should notice a second rise going into the thirteenth month, which is the point where the club's first wave of renewals hits the system. During that month, the club will add another wave of members into the system, as well as keep a certain number of members from the same month during the previous year who are still paying.

For example, the club might have signed up 100 new members during January. The following January, the club might have only 50 of those members still paying due to losses and normal retention. The club owner does, however, add another 100 members during this January, for a net of 50 extra members paying monthly dues:

January, 2006—100 new members added
– January, 2007—50 left after normal losses

Club has 50 from last January still in the system

An easier way to think about it is that the club added 100 members, but had only 50 left after adjustments. If it adds 100 new members, 50 cover the revenue from the lost members and the club is a total of net 50 ahead. In other words, the club now has 150 members paying monthly dues instead of the 100 it had from last year's memberships during the same month.

Opening during the typically slow months in the club business, such as May and June, will usually extend the break-even point out to about 10 months. The initial higher sales that come during the busier months are going to be lower during the slower months, which leads to a longer buildup of revenue from member payments.

The Key Concept in This Chapter

Modern presales are usually just 60 days or less. The old goal was to sell as many new memberships as you could and then collect the big membership dollars once you open.

Your goal should be to go into month 5 of your business with a healthy, satisfied membership rather than going into your first month with members who received large discounts many months before the club opened as incentives to join early. Be patient and go for the bigger membership dollars closer to opening.

IHRSA Tip—Corporate Challenge: Gaining the Competitive Advantage
—by Troy De Mond, M.A., and Len Kravitz, Ph.D.

As club owners face the daily challenges of signing up and retaining members, an often-overlooked strategy is to focus on corporate accounts. Businesses are always looking to improve employee productivity and retention, while simultaneously reducing costs such as health care premiums. In addition, health club memberships (or even discounts) are considered by employees to be valuable perks. This Tip details a successful corporate fitness initiative and highlights the recommended steps to follow on similar ventures.

Build from established relationships

It can be difficult for small clubs to establish an "in" with large corporations when trying to set up a corporate fitness program. Initially, focus on existing members who are in the upper management at their places of employment. Also, determine whether any club members have business relations with local corporations. It is preferable to collaborate with current members because they are using your facility, and are most likely satisfied with its offerings.

For example, the owner of Fitness on the Move Lifestyle Center in Fort Myers, Florida, enjoyed a positive club owner-to-client relationship with the CEO of Chico's FAS, Inc., whose world headquarters, with a staff of 700, is also located in Fort Myers. That CEO had exercised at the club for more than two years and, in conversations with club management, expressed a desire to motivate his employees to exercise—the "cue to action" that a business opportunity was ready to be cultivated.

The next step was to develop a marketing concept that would do two things: provide the company with a plan to create healthy opportunities for employees and develop a strategy for the club to ultimately convert these employees into revenue-producing members.

Launching the fitness challenge

The marketing concept developed in this case study was Chico's Fitness Challenge, which allowed employees to participate in a three-month exercise program at Fitness on the Move. With a large number of employees opting to participate, the club provided the company with a greatly reduced (by nearly 70 percent) corporate membership rate. The company offered a cash prize to the five employees who created the greatest fitness change during the challenge. Fitness on the Move also offered a one-year membership to each winner.

The company announced the challenge at its holiday party. Later, the company's administrative team sent broadcast emails to employees announcing the event. Employees who were already exercising at a gym were encouraged to participate. Employees were given three weeks to sign up.

It was decided that the winners would be the five individuals with the greatest percentage changes in their combined body fat and body weight loss. It was also made clear that any ties would be decided by awarding victory to the person with better club attendance during the challenge. This incentive promoted club usage and discouraged dieting alone without exercising.

Prior to the challenge, each participant completed a health history questionnaire and the club provided assessments of resting heart rate, blood pressure, body weight, and percent body fat. These meaningful health parameters served as objective variables, which are easily tracked over time, and are also of special interest to participants.

Getting off on the right foot

With the pre-testing complete, each participant met with a personal trainer for an initial consultation. This meeting provided direction on getting the most out of the personalized program. It also exposed the trainers to potential clients, thus increasing the trainers' (and club's) revenue opportunities. (If you have a large number of corporate challenge participants, try small group orientations with up to 10 people per session.) During each consultation, the trainer oriented the participants to the facility and provided instruction on cardiovascular conditioning, resistance exercise, and flexibility training.

Each participant was urged to exercise aerobically at least three days per week, for at least 20 minutes. Once a base fitness level was established over a three- to four-week period, participants increased their exercise duration to upward of 40 to 45 minutes per session. With continued improvement, another (optional) progressive overload recommendation included adding another day of cardiovascular exercise.

The personal training team provided instruction on selectorized weight equipment, which included a variety of exercises targeting the upper, lower, and core segments of the body. Participants began with a single-set program of moderate intensity, at least two days per week. They were instructed to increase the number of sets to two or three after two weeks. This initial session finished with a demonstration of flexibility exercises to do at the end of each workout. Lastly, the personal-training team encouraged participants to utilize additional club services such as nutritional counseling (with a registered dietitian).

The start-up follow-up

During the first month, the sales team monitored participation. After the first two weeks, any participant who did not visit the club received a phone call. During these conversations, a positive dialogue was used to encourage them to take advantage of the opportunity and to inform them that if they needed anything, the staff was ready to help. This conversation proved to be a powerful contributing factor to program participation.

At the 30-day mark, calls were made to those individuals with three or fewer check-ins. Participants were informed that enough time was still available to create positive health changes. After the 30-day mark, any nonparticipant was mailed a "thinking of you" card to let them know that they still had time to start the program.

After the first 30 days, the club provided the company's CEO with a progress report, which included an update of participation, attendance data, and positive changes already occurring with some participants. The CEO was encouraged to share this feedback with all employees to keep the challenge on their minds. In addition, the club's management posted some short-term success stories on the club's reader board, to acknowledge these participant leaders and to inspire others.

Each participant received a commemorative shirt, paid for by the company. An email announced that shirts could be picked up at the club, which provided another incentive to attract employees to the facility.

Sales team jump-start

After the first month, the club's membership team began to focus on converting participants into paying members. The company was invited to distribute (via email) a time-sensitive incentive offer to all employees (participants and nonparticipants), encouraging early club enrollment before the challenge ended. This email converted 20 percent of challenge participants into club members. A second email was sent to employees toward the end of this offer.

Everybody wins

The results of the post-testing assessments were inspiring, and many participants were eager to continue exercising at the club. During these assessments, the club's membership director was present to facilitate sign-ups.

A showy event announcing the winners from the fitness challenge was held, working collaboratively with the company's public relations department. Press releases were sent to local media sources announcing the big event. The five winners received their prizes at this event. Perhaps the biggest winner was Chico's FAS, Inc., which was rewarded with healthier, happier, and more productive employees.

Chico's fitness challenge overview

- 210 people checked in at least once
- 92 people used the club at least 12 times
- Check-ins totaled 3,374 (average 281/week or 47/day)
- 78 people were post-tested; they lost 540 pounds (average of 7/person)
- 65 people converted into paying members
- The greatest weight loss for a single participant was 44 pounds

Download handouts to accompany this Tip by visiting www.ihrsa.org/tips.

Troy De Mond, M.A., is the owner of Fitness on the Move Lifestyle Center. He can be reached via email at info@fitonmove.com. Len Kravitz, Ph.D., the program coordinator of exercise science and researcher at the University of New Mexico, can be reached via email at lkravitz@unm.edu.

Appendix A: IHRSA Resources

Congratulations on your decision to enter into the health club industry. This industry continues to outpace the growth of other industries, as more and more people choose regular exercise as a way of life.

As you dig in and develop your new business, you can increase your opportunity for success by choosing to align yourself with IHRSA, the International Health, Racquet and Sportsclub Association. Founded in 1981, IHRSA is the definitive voice of the global health club industry.

#1. As an IHRSA member, you'll know what's ahead of you.

Imagine having all the answers you need to set up and run your fitness business. With IHRSA on your side, you'll have an unmatched resource to ensure the success of your business, providing help and guidance for everything from staffing and statistics to legal issues, insurance, and even money-saving group purchasing.

#2. Acquiring financing is tough! As an IHRSA member, you won't be alone.

IHRSA's research reports, all vital for strategic planning and benchmarking, are invaluable for recruiting investors and/or obtaining financing. The following are just a few of the many financially helpful reports included in a developer membership (for a complete lists, visit ihrsa.org/developers):

- IHRSA's annual industry data survey, *Profiles of Success*, presents key information on club operations, finances and trends.

- IHRSA's annual *State of the Health Club Industry* reports on the internal and external factors that shape the health club industry.

- IHRSA's *Guide to the Health Club Industry for Lenders and Investors*, designed for you to share with your potential lenders, will help everyone understand the market conditions and operational details that will help your business succeed.

- IHRSA's *Guide to Bank Financing* advises club operators on how to make the best possible loan presentation to banks and helps them develop a proposal that will be favorably received and accepted.

- IHRSA's *120 Million by 2010, A Progress Report on the Fitness Industry's Plan for Growth* raises the bar from IHRSA's 1999 goal of 100 million health club members worldwide by 2010. This book provides insights into how some of the best-run club companies are achieving growth and why there will be, not 100 million, but 120 million health club members in 2010.

#3. As an IHRSA member, you'll have the industry's legal department in your corner.

Setting up a business needs to be done right the first time. Ignoring the laws, regulations, or consumer-protection statutes can ruin your business and bottom line. As an IHRSA member, you are only a phone call or email away from valuable information on membership, contracts, bonding, dealing with difficult members, addressing employee issues, ADA and OSHA requirements, privacy issues, and more. Check out www.ihrsa.org/state to read information specific to the laws in your state.

#4. Staffing doesn't have to be as hard as it seems.

Personnel issues are the number one frustration among club owners. Not only does IHRSA provide the industry's top career finder with www.activecareers.com, but IHRSA will also be your main resource for help and guidance on staff training, continuing education credits, compensation and benefits practices, job descriptions, internship manuals, noncompete agreements, employment law information, and much more.

#5. As an IHRSA member, you'll stay current on the latest industry news and how it impacts your business.

IHRSA is tapped in to the pulse of the fitness industry. You will find your membership an invaluable resource for keeping you up to date with industry news, programming and promotional ideas, new products and services, answers to your most frequently asked questions, consumer attitude statistics, trends, best practices from clubs around the world, and much more.

As an IHRSA developer member, you will have complete access to IHRSA's information and services through published reports, *Club Business Industry Magazine*, which is the fitness industry's magazine of record, special publications for entrepreneurs/independent club owners, access to the member-only areas of www.ihrsa.org and full-member access to IHRSA's research department.

- IHRSA has been collecting industry and consumer-related research for more than two decades. Visit www.ihrsa.org/research for more information.
- *Club Business International Magazine* (CBI) speaks to the specific concerns of running a successful health club.
- *Club Business for Entrepreneurs* is tailored specifically to owners and developers of small, independent U.S. health clubs.
- *Fitness Industry Technology* (F.I.T.) compares equipment features and pricing at-a-glance with this annual publication.
- e-Newsletters provide IHRSA members with specific targeted newsletters on

industry news, marketing tips, business resources, and more.

- *The Buyer$Mart* helps you find industry suppliers, and features product profiles, hot product news, and more.

#6. IHRSA's meetings and events provide education, inspiration, and motivation.

IHRSA produces and hosts a wide range of meetings and trade shows, all designed to help you learn as much as you can about the industry before you open your club. IHRSA members receive member pricing on all IHRSA educational events and special rates are available for first-time members.

- IHRSA's Annual International Convention and Trade Show is your best opportunity to experience the industry's best education and networking while seeing first-hand the industry's latest products, services and technologies. IHRSA members receive member pricing on convention registration packages with special rates offered to first-time members (www.ihrsa.org/convention).

- IHRSA's Annual Club Business Entrepreneur Conference is designed specifically for the owners and developers of smaller independently owned health and fitness clubs. At this conference, you'll not only learn from the industry's top "small-club business experts," but you'll also meet and network with club owners and developers going through the same experiences you are (www.ihrsa.org/conference).

- IHRSA's Annual Institute for Professional Club Management provides four full days of exceptional education led by expert faculty and outstanding networking and social opportunities. Attendance is limited to ensure graduate-level class sizes. Outstanding peer networking and social opportunities are abudant (www.ihrsa.org/institute).

- Visit www.ihrsa.org/meetings for a full list of IHRSA event dates and locations, including international and regional events.

To learn more or to become an IHRSA developer member, you can do one of the following:

- Return the questionnaire on page 215 by fax or mail.
- Call toll-free today at (800) 228-4772 (US & Canada) or (617) 951-0055 (international).
- Email membership@ihrsa.org.
- Visit www.ihrsa.org/developers.

Additional IHRSA Resources for Club Developers and/or Those Entering The Fitness Industry

Along with the following publications, the IHRSA Store offers MP3 recordings of selected session from the 2005 and 2006 International Conventions. DVDs of selected educational sessions from *IHRSA 2007, the 26th Annual International Convention and Trade Show* are available at www.ihrsastore.com.

***Profiles of Success* 2006, IHRSA's Annual Industry Data Survey:** The 2006 *Profiles of Success* provides detailed information about health and sportsclub operations, including data for club revenues, expenses, pricing, equipment purchasing, and more. Based upon IHRSA's annual Industry Data Survey of its North American membership, the 2006 report presents data from 2005 and 2004 in terms of both club type and club size, allowing for even more meaningful comparisons for individual clubs. Club owners, investors and developers continue to use this unique report to prepare business plans, determine the value of a club, and to obtain financing and investment. This product is included in an IHRSA developer membership and is available for purchase at www.ihrsastore.com.

Uniform System of Accounts for the Health, Racquet and Sportsclub Industry: This comprehensive guide to accounting procedures for clubs was published under the direction of industry CFOs and CPAs. Whether you are seeking financing or are simply interested in evaluating your performance against industry benchmarks, you need to ensure that your accounting system reflects the industry's best practices. This publication details the industry standard for revenue and expense recognition, provides a sample chart of accounts, explains how to calculate important ratios such as debt-to-equity, suggests a method of budgeting, and more. This product is included in an IHRSA developer membership and is available for purchase at www.ihrsastore.com.

IHRSA's Guide to The Health Club Industry for Lenders & Investors: Investors, though interested in the health club industry, often lack the reliable information required to make informed investment decisions. Now, however, all of the details and data that bankers, venture capitalists and others need to evaluate club investments are available in a single publication. This unique reference will be especially valuable to club owners who want to educate their current investors, or who are seeking new investors or refinancing. This product is included in an IHRSA developer membership and is available for purchase at www.ihrsastore.com.

IHRSA's Global Report on the State of the Health Club Industry: This book is the most comprehensive overview of the worldwide health and fitness industry available anywhere. Industry leaders representing all corners of the globe and all facets of the industry comment on the challenges and opportunities facing the industry. The

Global Report contains a directory of the major club companies worldwide, including financial information where available. This product is included in an IHRSA developer membership and is available for purchase at www.ihrsastore.com.

IHRSA Employee Compensation & Benefits Survey Results: This document, the most comprehensive survey of the North American health club industry's compensation and benefits practices, provides compensation information for 50 common job titles, with commission rates and benefits. Data is presented in terms of company revenues, geographic regions, and number of clubs operated. This product is included in an IHRSA developer membership and is available for purchase at www.ihrsastore.com.

F.I.T., IHRSA's Fitness Equipment and Buyers' Guide: With more than 1,000 product and service listings, this book is the industry's only comprehensive guide to commercial fitness equipment and other essential health club products and services. F.I.T. is designed to simplify the equipment-purchasing process. The material is organized by product category and accompanied by charts to allow for comparing of product features. This product is included in an IHRSA developer membership and is available for purchase at www.ihrsastore.com.

120 Million by 2010—The Industry's Plan for Growth: In 1999, IHRSA set a goal of 100 million health club members worldwide by 2010. In 2006, the bar was raised. This report analyzes the many changes in the fitness marketplace and customer demographics, and benchmarks how the industry is doing in meeting its original goal of 100 million members. Furthermore, it provides insights into how some of the best-run club companies are achieving growth. This publication is a must-read for anyone who wants to understand the factors influencing the health club marketplace and for club operators who want to expand their business in the years ahead. This product is included in an IHRSA developer membership and is available for purchase at www.ihrsastore.com.

Club Business for Entrepreneurs Quarterly Magazine: *Club Business for Entrepreneurs* is tailored specifically to the owners, operators, and developers of small, independent U.S. health clubs. This quarterly magazine and corresponding monthly e-newsletter will expose you to independent club operators who've gone through the same operational difficulties you're now facing as a club developer. This magazine is included in a developer membership. Call (800) 228-4772 or (617) 951-0055 or email ent@ihrsa.org for a free copy.

Club Business International (CBI) Monthly Magazine: Monthly issues of *CBI Magazine* will keep you up to date on the latest industry trends and the specific concerns of clubs, large and small. Club operators, whether new to the industry or industry veterans, prefer reading *CBI* to other industry trades by a large margin. This magazine is included in a developer membership. Call (800) 228-4772 or (617) 951-0055 or email cbi@ihrsa.org for a free copy.

IHRSA's Guide to Bank Financing: Bankers have specific expectations with respect to what they need to see before they will approve a loan. If those expectations are not met, a loan proposal has little chance of being accepted. This publication advises club operators and developers on how to make the best possible loan presentation to banks and helps them develop a proposal that will be favorably received. This product is included in an IHRSA developer membership and is available for purchase at www.ihrsastore.com.

Best of John McCarthy: Thoughts on Industry Growth, Competition, and the Club Business: John McCarthy, IHRSA's Executive Director Emeritus, shares a selection of his best writings since 2001. Sponsored by CheckFree and Cybex, these articles display McCarthy's wealth of knowledge and insightful perspective from his 25 years of service in the industry. This book is a valuable resource for anyone interested or invested in the health club industry.

Are you interested in the health club industry around the world? Read the most comprehensive overview of the Asia Pacific health club market to date in a first-of-its-kind publication, ***The 2006 IHRSA Asia Pacific Market Report: The Size and Scope of the Health Club Industry***. For the most comprehensive and authoritative source of data available on the European fitness market, purchase ***The 2006 IHRSA European Market Report***. It is a great tool for researchers, banks, investors, governments, insurance companies, club owners, and suppliers.

Save hundreds of dollars when buying multiple publications! Visit www.ihrsastore.com for more details.

Additional Resources

The National Fitness Business Alliance (NFBA)
800-726-3506

The NFBA is an alliance group formed to bring education to club owners near where they live and operate, and to offer products and support services for the independent club operator. The NFBA includes many of the biggest companies in the industry, which have banded together to make education easily accessible for any owner who wants to spend a few days working on his business without the cost of traveling across the country.

Thomas Plummer, founder of the NFBA, is the foremost educator and consultant in the fitness business. NFBA seminars attract more than 4,000 students annually and offer ideas to help you as an owner grow your business. He is also the author of the three biggest selling books in the fitness industry: *Making Money in the Fitness Business*, *The Business of Fitness* and *Anyone Can Sell*. NFBA offers a number of educational events throughout the year as part of the National Fitness Business Alliance, the International Health, Racquet and Sportsclub Association (IHRSA) and other organizations. For further information about Thomas Plummer, go to www.thomasplummer.net.

IHRSA Buyer$Mart

The IHRSA Buyer$Mart (www.ihrsa.org/buyersmart) brings the opportunity and excitement of an industry trade show right to your computer! You can find valuable products and services, conveniently—without leaving the comfort of your office. The Buyer$mart is IHRSA's free online buyer's resource, searchable by company, product, or service. Whenever you are looking for a company, product, or service offering, visit www.ihrsa.org/buyersmart to access a wealth of information and resources.

About the Author

Thomas Plummer has more than 25 years of experience in the fitness industry. He is the founder of the Thomas Plummer Company, which currently has eight full-time employees and does approximately 22 major seminars per year. He has also founded the National Fitness Business Alliance (NFBA), a group of industry vendors and suppliers who, with IHRSA, have banded together to provide education and tradeshows to the independent club owner.

Thomas Plummer is in front of more than 4,000 people a year, through numerous speaking engagements as a keynote speaker and event host. He is also the author of four books on the business of fitness, which have remained the bestselling books in the industry for almost 10 years. Due to the number of people who attend the seminars, coupled with the popularity of his books, many industry experts feel that Thomas Plummer is the most influential person working in the fitness industry today.

From 1985 to 1989, he became the vice president of marketing for American Service Finance, the largest third-party financial-service provider in the industry. Soon afterwards, he became the executive director of the National Health Club Association from 1989 to 1990, which was founded by the owner of American Service Finance to capture the independent market.

He created Thomas Plummer and Associates in 1991 and started a limited tour with industry sponsorship. In 2003, he reformed the company and moved it to Cape Cod, Massachusetts. The NFBA, which was founded in 2006, is currently the largest provider of education for the independent owner in the world.

Thomas attended Western Illinois University and then attended graduate school at the University of Arkansas. He started working in the martial arts (taekwondo) in 1976. He worked as a ski instructor in Colorado for 10 years, raced bicycles in the 1970s, reached a third-degree black belt in the 1980s, and loves hiking, music, and books. He currently lives on the Cape with his family, travels extensively, and is currently working on his next book project.

IHRSA Membership Questionnaire

Success By Association

Name of Club under Development: (leave blank if unknown)

_____

Owner/Developer: _____

E-Mail: _____

Mailing Address: _____

City: _____ State: _____ Zip/Postal Code: _____

Telephone: (___) _____ Fax #: (___) _____

Projected Opening Date: (leave blank if unknown) _____

Projected Club Type: (leave blank if unknown) _____

❏ I am not ready to join IHRSA yet, but I would like to learn more about IHRSA. The best way to reach me is: _____

❏ I am not ready to join IHRSA yet, but would like a complimentary subscription to "The Source" – IHRSA's monthly e-newsletter for club operator success. My email address is:

_____

❏ I am ready to join IHRSA as a Developer Member. My dues payment information is attached or below.

IHRSA's Annual Developer Membership dues are $950.00 per year.

For Developers in the six New England States, Developer Dues are $1,025 per year and also includes the many benefits of NEHRSA (The New England Health Racquet & Sportsclub Association) membership.

Amount enclosed: $_____

❏ Check Enclosed (U.S. Currency Only), made payable to: **IHRSA**

❏ Credit Card: ( ) MasterCard ( ) VISA ( ) American Express ( ) Discover

Number: __ __ __ __ - __ __ __ __ - __ __ __ __ - __ __ __ __

Expiration Date: _____

Cardholder Name (Please print or type): _____

Signature: _____ Date: _____

All IHRSA Members agree to abide by the IHRSA Club Member Code of Conduct:

As a member of IHRSA, I agree to operate my club(s) in the best interest of the consumer and the industry by:

- Treating each member as though the success of the club depends on that individual alone;
- Systematically upgrading our professional knowledge and awareness of new developments in the industry;
- Designing our facilities and programs with members' safety in mind;
- Continuing to increase the value and benefits of our services and programs;
- Providing public service programs to expand awareness of the benefits of regular exercise and sports;
- Refraining from illegal activities and deceptive sales practices;
- Delivering what we promise; and
- Conducting our business in a manner that commands the respect of the public for our industry and for the goals toward which we strive.

Other rates and membership packages are available. For more information on the benefits of IHRSA Membership, call or visit ihrsa.org/membership. Send this form back via fax to **617-951-0056** or mail to: **IHRSA Membership Department, 263 Summer Street Boston, MA 02210 USA**